ABOUT THE AUTHOR

Don Greene, PhD, was a nationally ranked
high school diver who graduated from West
Point. He served in the U.S. Army's Special
Forces as a Green Beret and went on to train
the San Diego Police S.W.A.T. team in
counterterrorism. Dr. Greene was the sports
psychologist for the U.S. Olympic Diving
Team, the World Championship Swimming
Team, Golf Digest Schools, and the Vail Ski
School. He lives in Manhattan.

Seven Skills for

Performing Your Best

Under Pressure—

A 21-Day

Programme

DON GREENE

FIGHT

YOUR

FEAR

AND WIN

Vermilion
LONDON

3 5 7 9 10 8 6 4 2

First published in 2001 by Broadway,
a division of Random House, Inc., New York.
This edition published in 2002 by Vermilion,
an imprint of Ebury Press,
Random House, 20 Vauxhall Bridge Road,
London SW1V 2SA
www.randomhouse.co.uk

Random House Australia (Pty) Limited
20 Alfred Street, Milsons Point, Sydney,
New South Wales 2061, Australia

Random House New Zealand Limited
18 Poland Road, Glenfield,
Auckland 10, New Zealand

Random House South Africa (Pty) Limited
Endulini, 5A Jubilee Road,
Parktown 2193, South Africa

The Random House Group Limited Reg. No. 954009

Designed by Nicola Ferguson

Papers used by Vermilion are natural, recyclable products made from
wood grown in sustainable forests.

Printed and bound by Mackays of Chatham, Chatham, Kent

A CIP catalogue record for this book is available from
the British Library

ISBN 0-09-188292-3

This is dedicated to my friend
Jerry Hunton,
for his unconditional support and encouragement
throughout my life.

ACKNOWLEDGMENTS

I would first like to express my deep appreciation to my mentors: John Barroncini, Doc Goldenberg, Colonel Robert Nye, Bob Nideffer, Bruce Ogilvie, Ron O'Brien, Peter Kostis, Joe Illick, and Julie Landsman. I'm grateful for your wisdom and guidance.

A special thanks goes to my wonderful friends: Jack Connor, Mary Jane O'Brien, Ed Castillano, Gina Browning, Laura Greenwald, Richard Chandler, Ann Baltz, David Aks, Elma Linz Kanefield, Lauren Schiff, David Geber, Ann Gabriel, Tom and Karen Kamp, Pete and Jackie Bloomer, Jerry Zampino, John and Mary Ann Connors, John and Jane Marcello, Nick and Cathy Bonarrigo, Eric and Linda Benham, Cesare Rosati, Joe Faraguna, Dick and Linda Measner, Bob and Manny Walton, Kevin Hanek, Bob Fox, and Josh Levine. Your caring is precious to me.

I'd like to voice my sincere appreciation to my musical colleagues:

Joseph Polisi, Stephen Clapp, Karen Wagner, Laurie Carter, Carol Adrian, Jane Gottlieb, David Wakefield, Tom Nazelli, Janet Kisson, Jane Rubinsky and Al Minor at the Juilliard School, and Michael Tilson Thomas, Candice Flores, Pat Nott, Fergus Scarfe, Michael Linville, and Doug Merilatt at the New World Symphony. Thank you for your acceptance and support of my work.

I offer my gratitude to Sylvie Bigar and Amanda Sweet at International Public Relations and Ralph Blumenthal at the *New York Times* for getting the ball rolling. Thanks to my agent Alex Smithline for hooking me up with Melinda Marshall and Broadway Books.

I feel so appreciate for the people who were generous enough to share both their time and personal stories: Ed McMahon, Peter Stewart, Bonnie Anderson, Steve Shelton, Jeff Hull, Michele Mitchell-Rocha, Greg Louganis, John Golden, Chris Leupold, Joey Mazzella, A. C. Morgan, Rob Endelman, Jeff Lee, Russ Bertram, and Polly Bergen. I also want to thank those who shared the intimate details of their journey, but whose identities I've promised to keep confidential. I could not have done the book without all of you.

I've been fortunate to spend some time lately with an impressive group of folks at Merrill Lynch. My heartfelt appreciation goes to Sara Karlen Lacombe, Amy Margolis, Mary Taylor, Joe Weldon, James Manfredonia, Matt Roberts, Will Bertsch, Patrick and Andrew Darcy, not to mention Henry, Scott, Eliza, Regina, Donna, Sean, Anthony, Frank, Jill, and Leo. Thanks for your warm welcome to Wall Street.

Since the inception of this project, I was blessed with an exceptional person: Melinda Marshall. I can only begin to thank you, Melinda, for sharing your talent, wisdom, and expertise—it was a pleasure and a joy.

I was also fortunate to have Suzanne Oaks and Claire Johnson, two of the most competent editors in the business, working on my manuscript. I can't thank you enough. To Toby Cox, Catherine Pollock, Debbie Stier, Brian Jones, and the rest of the Broadway staff, let me just say thanks.

Finally, let me express my deepest gratitude for my Mom and Dad, Uncle Joe, Uncle Len, Aunt Dot and Bill, and for your love.

CONTENTS

INTRODUCTION

The Seven Skills

In the pages to come, you'll be meeting:

* Anthony, a forty-four-year-old advertising executive who lacked the self-confidence and courage to pursue a career as a painter; today he's represented in several Manhattan galleries and has more invitations to show his work than he can accept.
* Bonnie Anderson, forty-five, a correspondent for CNN who feared doing live shots more than she feared War Zones; today, after a celebrated career as an on-location reporter Bonnie now oversees talent development of CNN's correspondents and an-

chors, helping them excel before the camera under any circumstances.

* Jeff, a thirty-three-year-old entrepreneur whose mortgage loan business unraveled as his wedding plans did; today he's an equity holder in a Silicon Valley start-up whose sales of computer routers have gone from $6 million to $50 million in three years.
* Julie, forty-eight, a mergers-and-acquisitions attorney who feared that her boss was out to get her; today she's a partner.

These are true success stories; they're among hundreds I've had a hand in during my career as a performance coach. I've chosen to highlight these four, along with some two dozen others, because they exemplify the sort of turnaround I imagine you yearn to achieve for yourself.

Maybe you haven't attained the success you feel your hard work should have brought you by now. Maybe you feel you have the talent to be tops in your field, but you can't seem to put that talent into play when it really counts. Or maybe you feel your potential just isn't being tapped. You're in a rut. You're spinning your wheels. You're getting nowhere.

But you're not keen on wasting time wallowing in self-pity, either. You're not interested in looking back to your childhood for reasons why you're at this impasse; you simply want to move forward. You don't want to be sabotaged by self-doubt any longer. You don't want to be paralyzed by panic or fear. You want a goal that will tap your full potential. And you want the courage and determination to go after that vision, no matter how "unrealistic" it may seem to others, no matter how much heat you have to endure, no matter how many setbacks you have to fight to overcome.

We're all fighting this fight on a daily basis. Life is like golf; golf, according to instructor Bob Toski, "is a nonviolent game played violently from within." We all feel the stress of performing under pressure; we all have known the agony of choking under that pressure. It is a basic human fear that in wanting something badly, we will not have what it takes to secure it for ourself when the opportunity presents itself. Yet it is this fear—and not a lack of talent—that does the most to undermine us. And the more competitive our culture becomes and the faster the pace of business, the more our fear of not being able to compete asserts itself.

This book can help. It encapsulates a program that has transformed people in all walks of life. The program is not a lifelong undertaking, however: In as little as three weeks you can acquire the skill that puts your dream within reach. That's no empty promise, but rather one based on rigorous research and extensive field testing. Nobody in the world has done as much as I have to bring out people's best, no matter what they do for a living.

For twenty years I've been a teacher, sports psychologist, and personal-best coach to thousands of athletes, police officers, and musicians. My clients have ranged from the U.S. Olympic diving team to the New World Symphony, from weekend skiers to professional golfers, from SWAT teams to Juilliard School graduates. What I learned about performance by working with such diverse achievers is that what gets in the way of performing optimally is universal. Clients who were held back from the success they deserved were held back by the same things, over and over. Their determination faltered. They couldn't control their nerves. They lacked self-confidence. They feared failure. They couldn't concentrate. Pressure paralyzed them. Mistakes undid them.

In designing a program to help each of them overcome these hurdles, I started to see the commonality in their struggle. There weren't hundreds of factors influencing performance outcome, as one would imagine. There were maybe twenty-four, and they could be categorized into seven sets as follows:

1. Determination

More a mind-set than a skill, determination is the strength of your intent. It consists of:

* *Intrinsic motivation,* or the inner drive that propels you toward a goal
* *Commitment,* or how vested you are in your mission
* *Will to succeed,* or the strength of your inner resolve, which may be influenced by such external motivations as the desire for money, power, or recognition

2. Energy

Optimal energy, or the level at which you perform best, isn't always the same as *performance energy*—the level at which you actually perform. For instance, you may do your best public speaking when you're relaxed and matter-of-fact, but under pressure to address a conference room full of strangers, your energy levels are off the charts. Under pressure, it's critical to be able to modulate your energy: to have either the *ability to relax* or, inversely, the *ability to energize* (if your optimal energy is high but you have trouble getting "up" for a performance).

3. Perspective

Your outlook shapes the outcome of your endeavors. It's affected by

* *Self-confidence,* or the way you feel about yourself or your abilities
* *Self-talk,* or the things you say, in your head, to yourself
* *Expectancy,* or the images you review or preview your mind's eye

4. Courage

The ability to act, despite fear, is courage. It requires you to have an *ability to risk*—to be proactive, to have a seize-the-initiative attitude rather than a defensive, wait-and-see one. Your *ability to risk defeat* reflects how much stomach you have for failure as an outcome—whether you can cope, or whether you're just too afraid of the unknown to risk it. Your *ability to risk success* measures how eagerly you embrace the undesirable consequences that come with success.

5. Focus

Focus has four aspects:

* *Presence* means the ability to stay in the here and now, and not allow your attention to wander to past events or jump ahead to future ones.
* *Intensity* refers to the amount of energy you're able to train on the object of your focus.
* *Duration* is a measure of how long you can sustain that intensity.
* *Mental quiet* is the ability to get past the distracting noise of cognitive thought.

6. Poise

Those who demonstrate ease under pressure are said to be poised. I use the term to describe, specifically, four high-pressure performances: *decision making, negotiating, presenting,* and *multitasking.*

7. Resilience

The ability to hang tough through adversity and persevere despite mistakes, setbacks, or outright failure is perhaps the most critical one in ensuring success. Resilience consists of the *ability to recover* from a mistake; the *ability to fight,* to stand your ground and not be victimized; and *mental toughness,* which is the ability to prevail, or get what you want, no matter what's thrown in your path.

In combination, these seven factors add up to success, provided talent is a given. And the equation holds true no matter what the performance arena. Anybody undertaking any challenge in any field can expect to triumph if armed with mastery in all seven areas.

I can offer you that mastery. Literally thousands of people have put my exercises to the test and found them effective. But better yet, I can customize a program of these exercises to address your particular shortfalls. I can recommend exactly what you need.

In the last few years I've refined an assessment tool that I first developed to help me customize training regimens for athletes. Called the Seven Skills Survey, it helps me zero in on a client's strengths and weaknesses such that we can dispense with months of psychological probing and exploratory therapy. I can determine, based on a client's scoring in seven different areas, just which exercises will be of most benefit.

If you were to score low in, say, the ability to risk, I wouldn't waste your time on exercises geared to improving your self-confidence. Fifteen minutes spent answering the questions on the survey might well bring you to an understanding of yourself that years of lying on a therapist's couch could not. My program is about creating the future, not trying to undo the past; about empowering you to make changes, not make excuses for what has already happened. Whatever success you envision, whatever goal you set yourself, I want you to see it is your choice. It is not up to chance.

No other self-improvement book on the market offers the depth of understanding or the range of practical exercises I offer in this volume. The seven factors themselves, plus their integration into a practical, effective program, is what makes my approach unique. You'll be able to tackle this program piecemeal, as the survey dictates just what you need to address and what you can afford to capitalize on. Each skill, in fact, is broken down into a twenty-one-day training regimen, to facilitate its mastery.

This point is worth emphasizing, because the underlying assumption of most self-improvement programs is that you can drop everything to focus on a total overhaul. That's absurd. No one who's on the road to success can afford to pull off and park for an indefinite period of repair. I'm not about to make over your personality or dictate your life choices. I'm not going to suggest you quit your day job, leave your wife, or abandon your kids. By the time we're through you may *decide* to make some rather significant changes—go back to school, switch careers, or give more or less to your personal life—but that's an end result, not a part of the process I've engineered. My job in these pages is to *empower* you to make the decisions you deem necessary to achieve your goals.

To be empowered, one must also be inspired. To that end I've crammed this book full of stories, real-life tales of change taken from both my highly visible and my virtually invisible groups of clients. You'll hear from Olympic athletes, champion golfers, Grand Prix race car drivers, and world-class musicians. You'll also hear from CEOs and entrepreneurs, venture capitalists and Wall Street traders, university professors and hospital administrators, salespeople and insurance execs, bankers and lawyers, anchorwomen and actresses, ministers and store managers, students and researchers. I've drawn, too, on my own experience—as a springboard diver, a West Point grad, an Airborne Ranger, a counterterrorist instructor, and a Green Beret.

But while I hope to entertain you, don't sit back and settle in. Get your pencil sharpened and prepare to do some work, because you don't come by the seven skills by nodding your head and saying, "Uh-huh—I get it." The only way to get it is to do it. There are logs to fill out, journals to write, actions to rehearse, images to visualize, diagrams to copy, maps to make, and charts to construct. Some of the work is mental; some is physical. It's not boot camp, but you need to be really serious about making the most of your natural abilities and hard-won experience. I assume you are. I assume you're *very* interested in finding out just how high you can fly, how far you can go, how many dreams you can realize.

I guarantee this guidebook will help you realize your dreams. But first, let's find out where you are and what you will need to complete your journey.

The Seven Skills Survey

Unless you want to wander in circles, no journey can begin without a map.

The ninety-six questions in the Seven Skills Survey are not a test, but a measure of where you stand in terms of the seven abilities I've found critical to success. I arrived at this survey after nine years' study of more than five thousand athletes and three thousand performing artists, and optimal performance training I conduct for management executives all over the country. Yet it's based, in concept, on the profiling tools used by my two mentors, leading sports psychologists Robert M. Nideffer, Ph.D., whose Test of Attentional and Interpersonal Style (TAIS) is the standard of the industry, and Bruce Ogilvie, Ph.D., whose Athletic Motivation Inventory (AMI) was the pioneering profiling tool in professional football and basketball and major league baseball.

While the Seven Skills Survey is an assessment tool, it's like none you've ever taken. It maps out your performance tendencies, not your personality traits. It takes no measure of neuroses or character defects; on the contrary, it's designed to show avenues for self-actualization you may never have considered. It will help you get to the heart of the matter—even if you think you already have all the answers.

One of my clients, a psychotherapist I'll call Susan, was highly skeptical of the survey's use as a diagnostic tool. As a trained therapist, she didn't trust anything so formulaic to accurately pinpoint her weaknesses. She already knew, she insisted, just what her problem was—a fear of public speaking. "I just want you to get me ready for this professional conference," she said. "It's a cut-and-dried thing."

I promised I would—on the condition she take the survey first.

Susan's nervous energy, as it turned out, wasn't the main reason for her presentation jitters. The survey identified three areas in which she needed help: her perspective, especially in terms of her negative self-talk; her resilience (she was more a victim than a fighter); and her focus, in all four aspects. She had great difficulty concentrating. In the five weeks before her conference, we met five times. We worked on her self-talk; I gave her an arsenal of focusing exercises. But the fact that she aced her conference appearance wasn't what gratified me most.

"I can't say I disagree with your survey's analysis," she granted me, somewhat begrudgingly, after we had discussed her scores. "Being unable to focus—the more I think about it, the more it rings true."

Like Susan, you can't afford to waste time working on skills that don't address your particular issues. You need to know which skills you're weakest in so that you can direct your energies efficiently.

The survey is designed to give you that knowledge. In less than twenty minutes you'll know where you are (which pieces of the success puzzle you've got in place), where you're headed (which pieces you'll need to go after), and what your route will be (which chapters of this book will help move you along the road to success).

You may come away from this exercise with more of a "big picture" take on your life than years of hourly sessions on a therapist's couch can give you—and for a whole lot less money, too.

But, then, this is a solution-oriented book, not one geared to exploring personal dysfunction. It's not a foray into your past, but a glimpse of your possible future. It's not about changing your personality; it's about changing the way you perform under pressure. It's about harnessing stress, instead of being debilitated by it. It's like that corny army advertisement: This is about learning to be all you can be.

How to Take the Survey

Relax.

Take a deep breath. Take several.

If you have access to the Internet, go to my Web site at *www.dongreene.com* and take the Seven Skills Survey on-line, because the Web site is set to score your responses and render your individual profile as soon as you complete it. Otherwise, complete the survey on the following pages. I've included directions on how to score your survey in Appendix H.

Answer the questions as honestly as you can. Don't obsess over any of them. The survey isn't a test you can pass or fail. Write down your gut response and try not to second-guess yourself.

The questions may seem repetitious. You may think you've already answered a question once, that there's been some mistake. There hasn't. Just keep writing down your most candid responses.

And remember, this is not a performance. No one is watching. No one will get hold of the results and pass judgment. This is between you and yourself. The more honest with yourself you can be in taking the survey, the more accurate the information you'll get back from it. Accurate guidance, in turn, will help you plot the quickest path through the rest of this book—and the shortest road to success.

SEVEN SKILLS SURVEY

Respond to each statement with one of the following:

5 = very true for me
4 = somewhat true
3 = sometimes/unsure
2 = not very true
1 = untrue for me

Example:

24   I have trouble focusing under pressure.   <u>4</u>

Answering **4** ("somewhat true") would indicate that you experience some difficulty focusing in stressful situations.

1 I have a strong inner drive to be my best. ____

2 Performing consistently well is very important to me. ____

3 I'm invested in being the best I can be. ____

4 I believe in my talent and abilities. ____

5 I start new projects with lots of energy. ____

6 It's easy for me to get "up" for important events. ____

7 Going into most situations, I expect to do well. ____

8 I have what it takes to make it. ____

9 I'm a creative problem solver. ____

10 I'm good at generating alternative approaches. ____

11 I present my ideas effectively to others. ____

12 I know how to keep an audience's attention. ____

13 I'm highly motivated from within. ____

14 I enjoy handling a number of important projects at once. ____

15 I'm willing to take the risks necessary to make it. ____

16 I do not fear success. ____

17 I have a strong will to succeed. ____

18 I respond well to difficult circumstances. ____

19 I have no trouble getting "up" for a challenge. ____

20 I function well at a high energy level. ____

21 I do my best when I'm feeling energized and "up." ____

22 I can think effectively even when things go wrong. ____

23 I keep my self-talk positive. ____

24 I view adverse conditions as opportunities. ____

25 I concentrate extremely well when I need to. ____

26 I'm able to quiet mental chatter. ____

27 I stay in the here and now when focusing on a task. ____

28 I have fought my way out of tough circumstances. ____

29 Public speaking can make me very anxious. ____

30 I feel nervous when performing in front of others. ____

31 I need to learn how to make better presentations. _____

32 I don't think that I come across well. _____

33 I have a strong fear of failure. _____

34 I frequently imagine the worst. _____

35 My approach to critical projects is one of caution. _____

36 It's difficult for me to get relaxed before important events. _____

37 I perform my best when I'm relaxed. _____

38 Even the thought of doing my best can make me anxious. _____

39 I wish I could do a better job of controlling my nerves. _____

40 Things never seem to go the way I'd like. _____

41 I have trouble striking deals. _____

42 I need to learn how to relax. _____

43 No matter how well I prepare, something always goes wrong. _____

44 I seem to get more than my share of bad breaks. _____

45 I tend to have doubts long before I even begin. _____

46 I worry constantly about messing up. _____

47 My decision making breaks down under pressure. _____

48 I function much better when I'm relaxed. _____

49 I don't think very efficiently when I'm pumped up. _____

50 I'd get off to a better start if I believed in myself more. _____

51 My nerves feel out of control. _____

52 I tend to begin critical tasks tentatively. _____

53 I need to be mentally tougher. _____

54 I get overwhelmed when there are too many things going on. _____

55 I have trouble focusing. _____

56 I do better when I work on one project at a time. _____

57 My mind races with instructions and critical comments. _____

58 I say things to myself that I'd never say to a friend. _____

59 I have a hard time quieting my mind. _____

60 I think too much about making mistakes. _____

61 I have a short attention span. ____

62 It's difficult keeping my mind on the task at hand. ____

63 My focus would not be described as intense. ____

64 Sometimes I just don't have enough energy. ____

65 I have trouble staying focused. ____

66 I tend to lose my concentration long before I'm done. ____

67 It takes me a while to get back on track after mistakes. ____

68 I really get down on myself. ____

69 I get very negative and critical. ____

70 One mistake can lead to a series of mishaps. ____

71 It's difficult getting my energy up after things go wrong. ____

72 Sometimes I feel that success isn't worth the effort it requires. ____

73 I'm afraid of some things that may come with success. ____

74 I don't always have to do my absolute best. ____

75 Sometimes success isn't all that it's supposed to be. ____

76 I'd probably do better if I were more motivated. ____

77 I feel out of touch with my goals and dreams. ____

78 I can bounce back from unfortunate circumstances.   _____

79 Difficult conditions bring out the fighter in me.   _____

80 Even if I'm tired, I can summon up my energy and rally.   _____

81 I know how to be mentally tough.   _____

82 I've dealt with failure many times in my life.   _____

83 I believe that things usually turn out for the best.   _____

84 It does not take me that long to get back on track.   _____

85 I think well under pressure.   _____

86 I can come up with several solutions to a problem.   _____

87 I'm not afraid of failing.   _____

88 I can juggle several important tasks at one time.   _____

89 I'm willing to push the envelope to see how good I can be.   _____

90 I embrace the consequences of doing my very best.   _____

91 I'm determined to be successful.   _____

92 I know how to focus intensely.   _____

93 I center myself in the present moment.   _____

94 I'm able to silence the chatter in my mind at will.   _____

95 I summon the courage to "go for it" no matter what.   _____

96 I focus on the task at hand until it's completed.   _____

**Please turn to Appendix H on p.220 to
find out how to score the survey.**

Interpreting Your Score

Each of the seven skills in the success equation—determination, energy, perspective, courage, focus, poise, and resilience—is comprised of three or four categories. Determination, for instance, consists of intrinsic motivation, commitment, and will to succeed; Focus is made up of presence, intensity, duration, and mental quiet. The scoring is not affected by the number of categories, however, because each skill score is the sum of their totals.

Scores fall within three ranges: low, midrange, and high, as indicated on your Seven Skills Profile.

An individual who scores high in all seven essential skills is someone who will perform to the best of his or her abilities under any and all circumstances. That is the rare individual. Most of us have at least one area in which we're weak, and another in which we can stand to improve. And our strengths and weaknesses change over time; what we score low in right now may prove to be one of our strengths down the road.

Taken as a whole, your scores indicate how driven you are, how nerves affect you, how you perceive your role in determining outcomes, how steely you are, how well you handle distractions, and how well you bounce back from mistakes or setbacks.

If you score high in any skill, give yourself a pat on the back. It's important not to take for granted what you do well. A strength is something to build on, something to derive courage from, a source of energy and confidence to tap. Think about what your strength has already helped you achieve, not what it obliges you to do in the future.

Now take an unflinching look at your low scores. Remember, they're not an indictment of your character, not a judgment of your worth. They simply describe how you function or fail to function in high-stakes situations at this particular time in your life. They shouldn't fill you with despair or a sense of failure; on the contrary, you should feel *relief,* because your work is cut out for you. Now that you know what's been thwarting your progress, you can tackle it. The tool for doing so rests in your hand.

The book is organized by skill set to make your task even easier. Each of the seven skills is given a chapter of its own; each chapter lays out a strategy by which you might acquire the set of skills discussed. While each chapter builds on those that have preceded it, you don't have to read this book cover-to-cover. Instead, use the survey scores to identify which chapters will close the gaps in your skill set. Need to work on your determination? Start with the next chapter. Having trouble pushing the envelope? Jump to Chapter Four, on courage. Finding focus to be your weakness? Move directly to Chapter Five.

But make sure that you start with the survey. With it, you'll have an accurate assessment of your situation. No journey can begin, no route can be plotted, no mission can be accomplished, without first determining where you stand at the outset.

Are you ready?

If you feel somewhat hesitant to embark on this journey, I understand. Many of my most successful clients started out reluctant to take the steps I recommended. It's human nature to fear the unknown. We'd rather wallow in misery that's familiar than step into uncharted territory that may be the Promised Land. But learning to perform at your best isn't root canal. I can assure you it's child's play in comparison to the complex coping mechanisms you've jury-rigged to get you this far.

You can make this journey. Follow my lead. I'll get you through it.

CHAPTER ONE

Determination: How to Set Goals and Go After Them

*Desire is the key to motivation, but it's the determination
and commitment to an unrelenting pursuit of your goal—
a commitment to excellence—that will enable you
to attain the success you seek.*

—MARIO ANDRETTI

One Sunday morning Ed McMahon, a client of mine who works on Wall Street, attended the 8:00 A.M. mass at his church without his wife and kids because he wanted to make the 10:00 A.M. tee-off time he'd set up with his golf buddies. He sat in the back, letting the priest's words wash over him, thinking about some of the reading he'd been doing from books I'd given him.

And suddenly, he was envisioning his funeral mass.

He could see his casket at the front of the church. It was as though he were suspended above it. *Who is sitting in the pews?* he wondered. *Who will deliver the eulogy? What will be said about me?*

"It caught me off-guard, I can tell you," he said. "I didn't go to mass to think that deep! It's programmed into me to just sit there and say thank you."

But in the month Ed and I had been working together, he'd been doing, in fact, quite a bit of deep thinking. At forty-six he was at the top of the pyramid, the senior guy on the equity trading desk at Merrill Lynch. He had a nice home and nice things. He was happily married, with four kids—two of them out of college plus ten- and seven-year-olds. On every front, he was doing enviably well. And yet he couldn't help but feel something was missing. He'd been the guy from Brooklyn without a college education who'd fought his way to the center of the ring. Now that he'd won, he was almost sorry the fight was over. The challenges he handled day-to-day felt predictable. More and more, it felt to him like he was just going through the motions, fast and furious but not really accomplishing anything. He didn't know what he'd rather be doing, though. That was the problem. He knew he was in a rut but couldn't jump-start himself out of it.

Sure enough, when Ed took the survey, his Determination score came up short. He was low on motivation. His commitment was flagging. And despite having achieved so much, without a new goal with real meaning, he lacked the will to succeed.

What Is Determination?

Determination is drive. It's the mind-set that impels you to make things happen. It's the strength, the power, of your intent. And it's the mental foundation on which the other six skills are built. No performance can go well without your having true grit—the determination to perform at the outermost edge of your capabilities. Success cannot be achieved without it.

People who lack determination usually do so for three reasons. One, they lack *intrinsic motivation*. Or to put it differently, they're missing the drive from within—the passion, the fire. That fire is ignited by a goal or desire. Those short on motivation have nothing driving them forward—no dream, no well-defined goal, no unmet desire or need.

Two, they're short on *commitment*. They're unable to vest themselves in the pursuit of any one thing. Commitment to a goal is rarely 100 percent—most of us have multiple priorities, after all, such as work, family, and a social/leisure life. But those lacking commitment can't even prioritize. They're immobilized by their options: They have so many, they can't pick one to start on. They're unable to decide which route to take because they can't decide which is the best one. Or they want to keep all their options open. Either way, they're stuck at the crossroads, incapable of taking action.

Finally, those who lack determination lack what I call *will to succeed*. This differs from *intrinsic motivation* in that it's more a function of the external pressures pulling us rather than our innermost dreams driving us. Perhaps we're seduced by our culture or socioeconomic group to make money or to gain status. Perhaps we want to prove something to our peers or win the approval of a certain group of people. Our will to succeed is affected by what we perceive to be others' definition of success.

Everybody knows what a lack of determination feels like: It feels like a rut. Like treading water. Like going through the motions. Like the engine is idling, instead of in gear.

But it seems that not many people know how to get out of this rut, how to come by the mind-set that moves mountains. Even the highly successful ones, sooner or later, run out of gas and have to wonder, *Is this it? Is this all there is?*

Many of my clients, like Ed McMahon, are at the top of what Abraham Maslow, founder of psychology's Human Potential Movement, termed the Hierarchy of Needs. They've taken care of baseline needs like food and warmth; they've moved beyond those to acquire physical security, like a house; they've managed to answer the human need to belong, to feel loved by family or friends, recognized by their peers; and they've even achieved a certain level of self-esteem. If you imagine these needs stacked up into a pyramid, then they are close to the pinnacle.

Yet like Ed, they're not all that happy, having achieved these things, because the fun is in the achieving, and now—well, *now what?* is the question they can't answer. David*, forty-one, an administrative department head, came to me because he thought his poor self-confidence was hurting his career; in fact, his career was hurting his confidence, because it wasn't what he wanted to do with his life. Career crises, marriage crises, crises of faith, crises of confidence—all are often just symptomatic of a fundamental absence of meaningful goals. While this abyss seems to yawn widest in midlife (because the quest for spouse, house, and kids is over and the career is on autopilot), it can open up at any time. Tom*, thirty-one, was a computer programmer who was floundering in midlevel management because he lacked a plan to move himself toward his dream of forming his own software company.

All these clients, you might say, were accustomed to feeling driven, but without something to shoot for, they couldn't summon any drive. Without something to aim for, they no longer enjoyed playing the game. It's as though they're out on a golf course with no holes. What's the point of driving the ball well? What's the point of even playing? Golf is defined by its holes. Without them, it's just hitting balls into the woods—not much fun in that.

There *is* something more to go after, however. There is one need they have yet to answer—what Maslow identified as the need to self-actualize.

History continues to be made because of the innate drive in humankind to stretch our limits, test our capacities, and exploit our talents to their fullest. Maslow studied highly functional individuals like Mahatma Gandhi and Albert Schweitzer, not the dysfunctional types Sigmund Freud documented, because he wanted to understand the

---

* Name and details of identity changed at client's request.

makeup of fully actualized individuals, those who continually achieved and redefined their goals in order to tap the furthest reaches of their potential. What set of qualities, what kind of psyche, he asked, led some people to keep pushing the envelope of the possible? And how could the rest of us come by that mind-set?

One of my life goals has been to translate Maslow's findings into concrete exercises that my clients can use to mobilize themselves out of ruts. And what I've found, in working with individuals poised on the brink of self-actualization, is that they often need help formulating their mission. Tapping one's full potential is a mission that's so big, so amorphous, and so *daunting* that most people don't know how to get a handle on it. But if we can break it down into a manageable task, our resolve strengthens. Our commitment grows. The power of our intent outguns the force of our fears. With clear goals to pursue, our intrinsic motivation fires up, and we find ourselves brimming with the will to succeed. I've seen this process happen with my clients over and over again.

Determination, in other words, is really a function of having clear goals—whether they're short-term assignments or long-term dreams. My goal in this chapter is to help you **figure out your long-term mission,** the so-called big picture; I've got two exercises that can help you zero in on your priorities. Then I'm going to give you **the goal-mapping tools to break it down into intermediate and short-term goals.** Once you have your goals and game plan in place, you will find that intrinsic motivation, commitment, and will to succeed develop all by themselves. Do the exercises, and you'll have both the dream to go after and the tools to make it come true.

But let's begin small. Let's get you in the habit of **setting small goals, working out short-term strategies, and racking up modest successes.** I want you to see just how powerful a clear goal and a straightforward game plan can be in terms of building your determination.

The Four-Point Field Order

What fostered my own determination was Ranger School, the two-month course in commando tactics that West Pointers are obliged to complete after graduation.

Ranger School was fifty-eight days of pure torture. We experienced every imaginable physical deprivation—no food, no rest, no dry clothing, no fires, no shelter—while patrolling hill and dale to engage aggressor forces. Typically, these patrols would begin with a jump out of an airplane or helicopter at dusk. We had military maps to help us gauge our location once we were on the ground. Whoever was designated as the patrol leader was given the mission and twenty minutes to come up with a game plan—what the army calls a Five-Point Field Order.

It always followed the same structure. It's such a useful way to transform the impossible or overwhelming into a plan of action that to this day I apply it to every challenge that threatens to immobilize me—although I've condensed the process somewhat, into a Four-Point Field Order. Here's how it goes:

1. Assess the situation. Dropped in a swamp or jungle, our first job was to send out a party and note key terrain features and landmarks so that we could find our location. Once we knew where we were, we could get a handle on the situation.

2. Determine the mission. It was usually an enemy outpost fifteen or twenty miles away across swampland, through dense forest, over mountains. We were to capture the enemy village with a minimum of casualties and free the captives by 0800 hours.

3. Figure out the execution and logistics. We had to come up with a strategy, a detailed plan by which we would accomplish the mission. We needed to factor in the enemy, major obstacles, and the time we planned to arrive at our attack position. We attended to details such as who would carry the mines, when we would eat (if at all), when we would sleep (never), and what our intermediate checkpoints were—where we'd assemble if we got split up.

4. Prepare for contingencies. Our mission was nonnegotiable. But we did formulate alternate strategies so that no matter what we encountered, we had a plan to enable us to move forward and stay on track. If we got cut off from one path by an assault, we had another one mapped out. We were ready for all contingencies so that no matter what, we'd accomplish the mission.

Now let's discuss these points as they apply to you. First: Have you assessed your situation? You can't go anywhere or accomplish anything until you figure out where you are. Only then will it become clear what kind of journey lies ahead, what kind of challenges you face, what kind of time frame you're working with. Do you know where you stand? Do you know where you're going? Do you know what you're up against?

If you completed the Seven Skills Survey, this work is already finished. You have gotten your bearings. You know where you stand in terms of what you have and what you need for the journey. You have a sense of your weaknesses, a firmer idea of your strengths. Great. We can move ahead to step two in the field order: Determine the mission.

You doubtless have many missions, but let's start with one that's limited in scope and duration. I can presume, since you're reading this book, that you want to groom yourself better for success. Let's say the survey has helped you identify two areas—courage and resilience—that need work. You're not a risk taker. Whether for reasons of nature or nurture, you've always played it safe, fearful that if you tried, and failed, you'd never recover. You probably can't see yourself becoming a risk taker anytime soon, either. But you may already see how your innate conservatism has held you back. Your play-it-safe strategy has peaked in terms of upward mobility. Your career, your life, and your satisfaction have all plateaued.

Your mission, then, should you decide to accept it (not that we were given this choice in Ranger School), is to find and take small steps past your comfort zone. Your goal is to change your reflex: to act on desire rather than allow fear of failure or fear of the unknown to paralyze you.

How are you going to achieve that?

We thus come to the execution phase of the field order. You need to figure out a strategy by which you can attain your goal, as well as a reasonable time frame and the tools to implement it. This book is in fact your method, your route. Since each chapter explores a factor in the success equation, you need to read up on the factors you're missing—let's say they are courage and resilience. The discussion in each chapter will help change your mind-set, which is the first leg of the route. The training exercises will help you build your courage muscle, toughen your skin, and provoke the fighter within you. Taken together, they'll inch you toward your goal—provided your timing is right. I can't stress enough how timing can affect the outcome of your mission; don't undertake this regimen until you have the energy, time, and freedom to apply yourself. You need time to read, time to jot down some notes, and time to perform the prescribed exercises on a daily basis. You'll need a minimum of three weeks for the exercises to help you acquire each skill.

Which brings us to the final step: contingency planning. Life is full of interruptions—children home sick, a broken ankle, a parent in need of full-time care, a new boss, a new project at work—but that doesn't mean you get off track with this program. Pick out a feasible time to resume your work if you have to suddenly put the program aside. Don't allow your goals to be jeopardized just because your schedule changes.

There are innumerable goals that you can substitute for the hypothetical one I've just discussed. Whether you want to lose ten pounds, get a raise, or have more fun in your life, the approach I've just spelled out remains the same. It gets easier and easier to apply it the more you practice doing so. While it doesn't matter how big or small, significant or insignificant, your goal, I'd suggest starting out with the simple, short-term variety so that you start piling up successful missions.

With each mission accomplished, the power of your intent grows.

In Ranger School we undertook our first couple of missions eager to succeed only because we knew we needed a certain number of successful patrols to graduate. We were motivated, that is, purely out of a desire to end the torture. But as it happened, with each successful patrol, our will to succeed at the next grew greater and greater until there was no longer any gap between intention and attainment. Whatever challenge they threw at us, we'd look at it and know it was a done deal. Our power of intent had become so great we were unstoppable.

In short, by feeding yourself a steady diet of clearly stated goals and using the field order to act on them, you build determination. You close the gap between wanting a certain outcome and making it happen.

Determining the Mission

What if you don't know the goal? What if you can't get a clear sense of the mission?

As I said, more often than not, step two of the Four-Point Field Order is the stumbling block. It was easy in Ranger School, because we were told the mission. In real life it's rarely spelled out. Some people go through their entire lives without ever knowing why they're doing what they're doing. They're on their deathbed before they figure out what mattered and what didn't, what choices they should have made, what choices they regret making.

You're not going to be one of them. I'm going to give you two exercises that will help you zero in on your mission while there's still time to accomplish it.

WHAT'S IN THE BUBBLE?

I developed this exercise when I was working with baritone Peter Stewart some years back.

Peter was at a crossroads. He felt in desperate need of a change in direction, but he didn't have a clear idea of the destination he'd rather head for. He loved his work, but it no longer seemed openended; it seemed that if he was to succeed, he had to wind up at the Met or on Broadway, and he resented the narrowness of those options. His personal life seemed stagnant, too: He was in a relationship he knew wasn't going anywhere but in which he felt powerless to make changes.

As long as Peter was singing with an ensemble or cramming to learn the score for his next performance, he didn't feel any angst. He was consumed by his work, enough to feel he was making progress so long as he was on stage somewhere. But the seasonal nature of his work wouldn't allow him to stay on stage. He couldn't remain caught up in the intensity of a production, because inevitably, it came to an end. There would follow months of downtime. And during these slack periods, his life felt directionless. He didn't know where he should direct his energies; he hardly had any to direct. He had hardly the motivation to get out of bed.

"I don't know what's next," Peter admitted at the cast party celebrating the end of the production. "I'm completely at a loss. I just want to hibernate."

I assured him everybody felt this way at one time or another. Even the most driven, goal-oriented people I'd known—Olympic medalists and Grand Prix champions—hit this kind of dead zone, this place of zero motivation. It wasn't a bad thing, this gnawing sense of stagnation. They'd hit it after reaching the medals and trophies they'd sought after so hard, so long. It signaled only that it was time to come up with new goals, a new mission.

No one ever gets done with goal setting, I told Peter, no matter how many goals they reach. Goals define us. They keep us motivated. They give our lives meaning. And without them we stagnate.

I had Peter brainstorm all the things that he wanted out of life, from the petty to the sublime. This could mean more money, a bigger apartment, or a new agent. Or it could mean a new kind of singing tour, a new lover, a change of careers. He wasn't to edit his list or impose judgment on it in any way. Not at first.

Next, I told him, imagine a bubble, the kind you used to blow out of a plastic wand when you were a kid. This bubble is bigger, but just as fragile; you can't stuff everything on your wish list into it or it will burst. You allow into it only what really matters to you, only what truly excites you, only what you would choose above all the other things on the list if forced to prioritize. The bubble is for your dreams. No one else's.

In creating this bubble, this open space in which to allow your heart's desire, don't be surprised, I added, to find any number of "shoulds" and "coulds" rushing in to claim the space. Nature abhors a vacuum. Lots of things that are appealing but not truly inspiring will vie for the space, but if you let them into the bubble, you only crowd your agenda and dilute the energy you can devote to any one of them. Don't let goals you think you should go after, or could enjoy having, crowd the one that really sparks your drive. The idea is to keep out all but the truly fulfilling, no matter what others may think of your goal and no matter how unlikely its attainment may seem.

Peter found this exercise surprisingly difficult. "Automatically, I put down some shoulds—as in, 'I want to sing at the Met.' I don't really want to, but that's what the world has conditioned me to think. It's amazing how automatically I lie to myself."

Once he eliminated the shoulds, Peter said, he had to tackle all the coulds. "There are lots of things I *could* enjoy doing," he explained. "The question becomes one of energy. If I'm going to succeed, I'm going to need a lot of it set aside for my pursuit. Do I want to fritter away precious time and energy going after a bunch of things I don't really care about?"

Peter finally honed the list down to three things he felt worthy of his total commitment: a world tour with a renowned composer; a CD recording; and a committed relationship. It was a process of elimination that took him weeks, because other things kept creeping into the bubble. But it was work that more than rewarded him, because since then—in the three years since he committed to pursuing those three goals—he has accomplished all of them.

We met again when he returned from his international tour with

Philip Glass (a tour whose highlights can be heard on CD, featuring Peter). At the time, he was committing to memory a new score for a concert in France, after which he planned to reward himself by taking his new bride to dinner in Paris. He wasn't exactly in a dead zone; he didn't intend to let himself get there. Instead, he wanted to get under way setting new goals for himself, new ways to stretch his definition of success, new paths to explore and feel excited about. He had seen for himself the way a clear mission could hone his power of intent until there was no gap between desire and attainment.

"The whole exercise makes you realize you can have the life of your choosing," he commented, "because you already do: You have, right now, the life you created for yourself. It reflects your choices so far. Only, you don't have to stick with what you've chosen. You can make new choices. And just the act of making them fills you with the determination to go after them."

IT'S YOUR FUNERAL

This second exercise is a bit more daunting, but it does tend to get right to the heart of the matter. I came across it several years ago in Wayne Dyer's cassette series *The Awakened Life*. The idea is to fast-forward, with your imagination, to your deathbed or your memorial service.

Remember the movie *Ghost*? Patrick Swayze is killed in a plot his best friend orchestrates to divest the investment bank where they both work of millions of dollars. But Swayze doesn't totally check out: Death puts him in a kind of limbo between the now and hereafter, allowing him to see all that he's lost—a lucrative job, an awesome SoHo loft, and a gorgeous girlfriend (Demi Moore) who cherished him. It's the loss of Demi that really causes him anguish, because he quickly learns he was betrayed over money. Demi was his one true thing, yet he had taken her love for granted. He hadn't been able to commit. He hadn't been able to bring himself to say, "I love you."

Now he's determined to say it—and that's the irony, because he can't get through to Demi, not even via a "medium" (Whoopi Goldberg), because Demi refuses to believe what she hears. He can't even protect her, because he can't move matter.

Then he meets up with a ghost in the subway who doesn't suffer the same limitations. This guy can break glass; Swayze can't even move a bottle cap. "It's all up here," says the ghoul, tapping his temple. "It's all in how bad you want it. You've got to use your will—your anger, your passion—to get it."

It's the power of intent he's talking about—a power that Swayze learns to tap only after he's been robbed of all others. By the end of the movie, he gets through to Demi. She can feel and hear him, though she can't see him. He tells her what he most wanted to say, what she most wanted to hear. But it's not the spirit world that gives him this power of mind over matter: It's knowing what he wants and committing himself to it 100 percent.

As I've said, there's nothing like death to give us insight on our lives. But if you can *imagine* yourself dead, now, while there's still plenty of time to act on the goals that become clear, then there's no need to lose everything in order to figure out your truest desire and start going after it.

This is what Ed McMahon was doing that Sunday morning before his golf game. He imagined himself laid out in a pine box (mahogany, actually) there at the front of the church, in the middle of his own funeral service. It was as though he were attending as a friend or family member, there in the back pew. He wasn't in a position to judge his own life; now it was up to whoever delivered his eulogy to do that. Who could he envision doing that? And what did he imagine would be said? Would he want his eulogy to be an inventory of the stuff he'd accumulated? A list of the houses, the cars, the money he'd made?

All that means nothing in terms of what kind of person I am, he re-alized. But if not, what then?

In the end, Ed couldn't imagine what it was he hoped to *hear* about himself at his funeral. But he did know whom he wanted to see seated in the pews. And he knew what he most wanted to see on their faces: smiles. "The kind of smile," he elaborated, "that said they really *knew* me."

It was a breakthrough. He didn't leave the church with a clear goal in mind, but he felt he knew for sure what he *didn't* want to spend his time pursuing. He didn't need, or want, a tonier address, another vacation home, a flashier car. The goal wasn't to accumu-late more wealth, power, and prestige—he'd been there, done that. He didn't regret his past choices. He just wanted to go forward making different ones.

"None of it's been a waste," he told me. "I needed the last forty-six years to get me to this point. I have a new awareness of what's important—and it's right in front of me."

Gradually, over about three weeks, we took that awareness and turned it into a mission. Ed wasn't about to quit his job and run a homeless shelter, or retire and take long walks on the beach with his wife. But neither was he going to commit his energies to going farther up the corporate ladder to claim the brass ring. He wanted balance in his life. He'd learned a lot since the birth of his first two kids; he wanted to appreciate the second two more. He also wanted a real challenge at work, something beyond just continually beef-ing up the bottom line. He realized he wanted to have a substan-tive impact on the lives of all the people who reported to him on the trading floor.

"We waste a lot of time here getting stuck on the little stuff," he said to me, gesturing to the traders bustling about and yelling across the bank upon bank of computer-laden desks. "We get caught up in the markets, caught up in the politics, until we're just busy-busy, rushing around like waitresses in a diner. We don't even know what we want anymore. No one can step back and see the big picture—

that it's not about money, or title, or what kind of car you drive or house you live in."

Ed's goal, in short, is to get his team where he is now: perceiving priorities, achieving balance, finding meaning in their lives instead of getting lost in the trappings.

"I have an opportunity here to make a real difference," he reflects. "It's like that line in *Illusions* [the book by Richard Bach I gave him to read]: 'You teach best what you most need to learn.' "

Figuring Out the Execution

Zero in on your destination, and you take the first step toward attaining it. A goal is what sparks motivation.

Now, however, you need a game plan, a strategy by which you can achieve your dream, step by step. It's all too easy to feel overwhelmed looking at the big picture. It's all to easy for that motivational spark to get snuffed out. The way to build motivation, to feed the spark until it becomes a raging inferno, is to map out your goals in long-term, intermediate, and short-term assignments.

GOAL MAPPING

Below you'll see two tables. They're taken from my goal-setting work with Tom, the computer programmer who was a program director at a major metropolitan library. Tom knew what his heart's desire was; he just didn't know how to go after it. Tom liked the people he worked with, and even his work, but his ambition had nothing to do with management. For years he'd been developing his expertise as a computer software and Web site designer, and recently he'd written a program that he felt might revolutionize the way in which large municipal libraries managed the payroll and benefits for all their part-time, full-time, temporary, and permanent staff. He'd gotten the interest of his employer; he could foresee a

INTERNET NETWORK FOR LIBRARIES			
TIME FRAME	THE LOGISTICS *The Nuts and Bolts*	THE EXECUTION *The Way*	THE MISSION *The Destination*
January 2001			Have 2–3 signed contracts
June 2000		Jump out of Nest	Start my own software company
Fall 1999	Put Web site together to promote software	Test the waters 5 deals in the pipeline	Create serious interest with clients
August 1999	Software ready to go to conference	Kick-ass presentation Slick brochure	Generate lots of interest in software
July 1999	Prepare presentation Design and print brochure		

business in which he contracted with libraries nationwide to supply his software and oversee its application. With as few as two or three contracts, Tom would be making enough money to leave his day job. His wife would no longer have to work, allowing her to devote herself full-time to raising their two-year-old daughter. And he could work from home—a lifestyle choice he'd yearned for since taking up computers on the side in college.

His mission, in a year and a half, was to get two or three signed contracts in hand. We wrote that in the upper corner next to the date that he estimated would give him a reasonable time frame. From that mission statement, we worked backward (or down) to determine what he'd need to do to reach that goal.

But in the course of doing the strategizing, Tom realized there was something even more compelling that he wanted to work toward. As his business grew and his client list expanded, he could foresee designing a network, not unlike AOL, to serve the library world. It could serve as a nationwide job clearinghouse. It could offer a speaker's bureau. It could spotlight successful youth programs, book clubs, art exhibitions, fund-raising events, and book sales. Any new developments in library science or technology would rely on it for nationwide distribution. And it might utterly change the way library personnel sourced new titles, videos, talking books, large-print and out-of-print books, microfiche, and computer hardware.

This vision wasn't so much a new mission as an outgrowth of his original one, so we scrawled it in above. The network idea simply became his five-year plan, whereas running his own business remained the eighteen-month plan. And nailing down a few contracts defined the execution.

With the ultimate goals now in place, I asked Tom to back up from them one step. What needed to be in place in order for him to be placed on retainer by two or three libraries?

Well, he'd need to have lots of serious interest, maybe five deals in the pipeline.

And to get those?

He'd have to generate widespread interest in his product.

You can see, under "The Mission," how Tom's answers defined his intermediate goals. Moving down from the top, each step was assigned a time frame. We determined that Tom's first mission—to get the word out, to generate lots of interest—should happen in August, a month hence from our discussion, because a conference of library administrators taking place that month would give him the perfect opportunity to present his product.

Then we worked across from that deadline to determine the strategy ("The Execution") by which he'd reach it. Look at the strategy goal to the right of "lots of interest": To maximize the opportunity the conference gave him, Tom realized he'd have to give a kick-ass presentation. And he'd need to follow up that presentation with a slick brochure outlining his product for his audience to take home and mull over.

Since Tom wasn't ready to do either, he had his work cut out for him over the next four weeks. He needed to prepare a pitch, brush up on his presentation skills, and get a brochure written, designed, and printed. These were his structural goals, the nuts and bolts that would uphold his dream, bolt by bolt, from the bottom up. While the table doesn't go into detail on how he tended to these tasks, we did break down the four-week time frame into short assignments. For instance, he spent the first two weeks getting his brochure together, because the printer had to have his copy and graphics by mid-July in order to have a brochure ready in time for the conference.

This was our tactic with each intermediate goal, working up from the bottom. By the fall, for instance, Tom knew he needed to get feedback on his product idea, so his strategy involved following up on the conference with calls and further promoting his software product with a Web site. By late fall or the end of the year, in order to get a few deals going, he expected he'd have to make on-site visits to learn what his potential clients needed in the way of special adaptations and then get them written into his software. And by the new year, in order to get clients to sign on the dotted line, he knew he'd need to come up with a demo he could e-mail out, showing his customization, proving his product's merit. With a few

TIME FRAME	THE LOGISTICS *The Nuts and Bolts*	THE EXECUTION *The Way*	THE MISSION *The Destination*
January 2004			Internet network for libraries
January 2001		Nail down 2–3 library contracts	In business for myself Work at home
June 2000	Produce demo software and e-mail it to prospective clients	Get 1 or 2 library contracts with libraries	Start my own company Jump out of nest
December 1999	Rewrite software for special needs of clients	Make on-site visits Deliver software to them	Convince 1 or 2 major clients about software
Fall 1999	Finish Web site to promote the software	Follow-up phone calls from conference	Create serious interest with major clients
August 1999	Software ready to go for conference	Kick-ass presentation Good brochure	Create lots of interest in software at conference
July 1999	Prepare presentation Design and print brochure		

of these contracts in hand, he could fully expect to be in business for himself by the following January.

Now, as you can imagine, our first draft underwent some refining. As Tom got under way, structure and strategy and mission goals became clearer to him. If you look at the table on the previous page, you can see how he moved things around.

Don't be afraid to do the same. If you've ever drawn a map for someone, you know how hard it is to get it right the first time. More often than not, you find you run off the edge of the paper before you get to the part that requires the most explaining, or you fail to get the scale right the first go-round. Goal setting is similar;

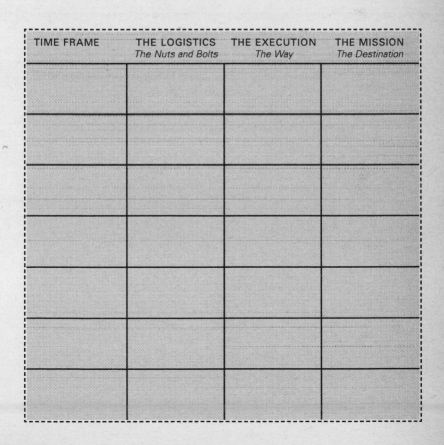

TIME FRAME	THE LOGISTICS *The Nuts and Bolts*	THE EXECUTION *The Way*	THE MISSION *The Destination*

it's more art than science. You're doing your best to capture on paper a route you can only imagine.

Start with one of your dreams. Write it down in the upper right-hand corner of this chart. What you need to do to get there can be overwhelming, so you don't start with that. Start with the nuts and bolts, the structural goals, the day-to-day ones, because they're manageable.

In fact, having determined your ultimate mission and laid out the path by which you might accomplish it, including all the logistics, you're done with the really tough work.

Now it's a matter of putting one foot in front of the other.

Prepare for Contingencies

Your goal or mission, as I've said, is nonnegotiable. As long as it remains in the bubble, as long as it inspires, excites, and beckons, it is to be held sacred and inviolable. That means that no matter what happens en route to your destination, you remain committed to reaching it. You will not be deterred.

But that doesn't mean you won't be detoured.

There is the very likely possibility that, in pursuing your goals, you will find that the road is not how you imagined it. There will be roadblocks, and you will be forced to change your strategy in order to get around them. This is where determination involves a degree of flexibility. While it's important to be rigid in your commitment to your goal, it's even more essential to be flexible in terms of the strategy you rely on to reach it. The best route to realizing your dreams may not, in fact, be the straightest one. Be ready to adapt. Be ready to devise a detour.

I saw the value in this while working with a woman we'll call Aileen*. For fifteen years, Aileen had been utterly committed to her career as an actress. She'd landed a few ongoing roles in daytime television; she'd had some success nailing roles in sitcoms that failed; and she'd been a movie star in France for the five years she lived abroad.

But at thirty-four she felt she needed some balance in her life, something to focus on other than her next role, because all that focus heaped on one thing wasn't helping her in achieving it. If anything, obsessing about her chances for success got in the way of attaining it.

"It makes no sense to think about an audition twenty-four hours a day," she told me. "You can only prepare so much. And no matter how good your technique, it all comes down to this one person liking you."

So Aileen took on a part-time job at a major department store as a makeup consultant. It was only eighteen hours a week; she had plenty of time to continue with her acting classes and enough flexibility to keep auditioning. It was just enough of a break, and enough of a departure from the acting world, to relieve some of the stress she'd been feeling.

But the job did more than take her mind off auditions. Aileen learned she was good at it—good at interacting with strangers, good at working with management, good at handling herself in a corporate environment. Within six months, without expending any real effort, she was promoted to manager.

"That taught me something about going after goals," she said. "I learned that if I take off the stress of having to get the prize—if I just work out of love for what I'm doing—then the prize comes to me."

The increase in status and pay gave Aileen a confidence, a surer sense of herself, that she could never get from acting. "I have people under me," she explained, "and I find I'm good at listening to them, good at getting them to give their best. I'm finding talents I never knew I had, and the confidence that it brings me spills over into my acting."

Last we spoke, Aileen was mulling over another promotion—one that would demand more hours from her.

"Some people would insist I can't go after my dream role if I'm working forty hours a week as a store manager," she reflected. "They would say I have to give one hundred percent to my acting. And when I was nineteen, just pursuing acting was the right thing to do.

"But now that I'm in my thirties, I see it differently," she continued. "Why can't I have a more rounded life and still keep the dream alive? I'm staying true to what makes me happy, only I'm taking a more balanced approach right now. I can choose that balance. I can make it fifty-fifty, or twenty-five/seventy-five—or even seventy-five/twenty-five. Because who knows? Having added responsibility at one job might give me the cutting edge I need to succeed at the other!"

Remember, your strategy, like your goal, is your own. There is no "right" way; there is only the route that works for you. And only you can determine what adjustments, what adaptations, must be made in order to stay on course even when the road chosen is blocked.

So be firm about your strategy at the outset, but remain open to course changes as you progress. If you need a little guidance, I've included a Determination Plan in the back of the book as Appendix A, where you can chart your own progress. You may reach your goal sooner than you thought, in a way you never imagined possible.

SUMMARY

Perhaps no other quality is quite so critical to success as determination. Without it, not even sheer talent or excellent connections can propel you to the top of your field. It is the power of your intent—**a combination of intrinsic motivation, commitment, and the will to succeed**—that **puts your heart's desires within reach,** regardless of obstacles. But building that power of intent demands you **have clear goals** or desires to pursue **and a plan** by which to attain them.

- **The Four-Point Field Order** is useful in **organizing your thoughts or plan of attack.** It works best once you know your mission.
- **"What's in the Bubble?"** If you're overwhelmed with options and can't decide which to go after, this can help you **prioritize.**
- **"It's Your Funeral":** If you're really in a rut and need to rediscover a meaningful direction for your life, this will help **put it into focus.**
- **Goal mapping** will help you **plot the short-term and intermediate steps** that, over a set period of time, will result in achieving your long-term vision.

Finally, it's important to understand that the more rigidly you define success, the more flexible you need to be in terms of your map. *Don't let unexpected roadblocks keep you from your goal.* Allow your determination to lead you down alternate routes, if that's what it takes.

Remember, turn to Appendix A for your own Determination Plan.

CHAPTER TWO

Energy: How to Control the Stress Response

The real difference between men is energy.
—R. BUCKMINSTER FULLER

Every two weeks, Audrey*, a thirty-seven-year-old marketing researcher for a Fortune 500 company, was called on to present her findings. Sometimes the meetings were informal roundtables with her department to discuss focus group results or plan strategies for gathering data. But frequently, she and other members of her department shared their information with high-level executives outside of marketing, executives who would make decisions worth hundreds of thousands of dollars based on the research they heard.

Making these presentations was an integral part of Audrey's job. There was no getting out of it.

And yet every time Audrey had to stand and deliver, she thought she was going to die.

"My heart was pounding so hard it felt like it was expanding into my entire body," she told me. "The faster my heart raced, the quicker and shorter my breathing got, until I thought I'd pass out from hyperventilating. I was so palpably nervous I could look at my hands and see the tops of my forearms pulsating."

The curious thing, she added, was that for the longest time, she actually thought she was good at making presentations.

"I wasn't shy. I didn't have a complex that I knew of," she explained. "But the truth was, for years I'd never had to do it! I must have been avoiding it subconsciously—until this job put me on the spot."

Audrey tried all the usual tactics. She bought books on overcoming her fear of public speaking. She read up on how to polish her presentation skills. She sought out colleagues she thought might be sympathetic, and shared with them what she went through, hoping they might offer her some pointers. But while she was offered a lot of empathy, no one could really help her.

Her torment grew. "Three, four days after I'd gone before the group, I'd get literally sick," she recalled. "All that adrenaline and terror just broke me down physically. I was spiraling down, down, down. I felt if I didn't solve this crisis soon, I was going to be out of a job."

What Is Energy?

Audrey's response to the stress of performing—in her case, making a presentation to her peers and superiors—is classic. She's panic-stricken, not just when she stands up to speak, but well before she even enters the room, before, even, she gets to work.

You probably know the feeling, even if you have no problem making presentations. Maybe for you it arises from having to close a deal—a really critical one, one with the power to make or break your business. Maybe it's pulling together a marketing study, a legal brief, or a program when you're behind deadline. Maybe it's meeting a sales quota when the fate of your division or product line hangs on it. Or maybe it's performing a tricky procedure, one with a lot of downside if you don't do it exactly right on the first try.

I know you know what panic is. But I'm going to redefine it for you—in terms of *energy*.

Look at the chart below. It's a visual representation of the four kinds of energy people feel when they go into a performance. I've adapted it from one sketched by Jim Loehr in his book for tennis players, *The New Toughness Training for Sports*. The horizontal axis moves from the negative to the positive; the vertical, from low to high. Panic, you'll note, falls into that upper left-hand zone—which, on this chart, can be described as *high negative energy*. But it should be clear that energy, and a lot of it, can be a positive thing. Think how often an optimal performance is described in terms of high energy: The person was "up," or "psyched," or "pumped," or "hot," or simply "on." It's the same energy *level* as panic, but it's a different quality of energy, which can be harnessed and controlled, so that it feels *good*. This is *high positive energy*, and for many of my clients, this is the energy zone in which they perform optimally.

Some people perform optimally only when they are positive but relaxed—in the lower right zone. They experience *low positive energy;*

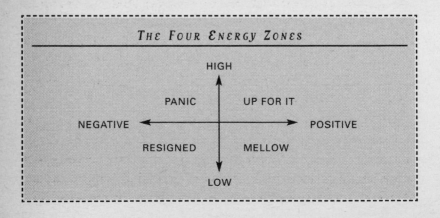

THE FOUR ENERGY ZONES

HIGH

PANIC   UP FOR IT

NEGATIVE ←——————→ POSITIVE

RESIGNED   MELLOW

LOW

they're mellow. Olympic diver Michelle Mitchell-Rocha, whom we'll talk about later in the book, is one of them. She did her best when she was matter-of-fact about performing, not when she was excited.

As it turned out, Audrey, too, did her best work when she was relatively relaxed. Her *optimal energy* was positive but low. But unfortunately for Audrey, her *performance energy* was in a completely different zone. When she's called upon to perform under pressure, to make presentations, she's not relaxed, but hyper. She's feeling panicky, not positive. Her performance energy should be in the same zone as her optimal energy. But it isn't. There's quite a distance between the two. In the survey this sort of problem showed up as a sizable gap in scores between her OE and PE.

Audrey's survey also indicated, not surprisingly, that she lacked the *ability to relax*—the ability to pipe down to her optimal, relaxed state at will. Clearly, as we've seen, she could not get a grip when she needed it most. In this respect, Audrey is typical.

And yet even people whose energy levels go off the charts when confronted with the pressure to perform don't always have the *ability to energize*—which is the ability to get psyched no matter how tired or down in the dumps they may be when it's their turn to deliver.

In short, unlike all the other skill categories, *scoring* low in Energy doesn't mean you *are* low in energy. It's simply a measure of the gap between your optimal energy level and the level at which you typically perform under stress (performance energy). And that, in turn, is usually a reflection of your inability to modulate your energy at will, either up or down. If stress typically makes you panic, this means you need to learn to relax, or modulate your energy down. Conversely, if stress brings out a defeatist attitude in you, a resignation—the lower left zone—you need to learn how to rally.

Either way, your **stress response** controls you. In this chapter you will learn how to control it. The technique is called **centering,** and it will prove to be a fundamental tool in **managing your energy and controlling your focus under pressure.** Derived from the martial art of aikido, this seven-step process can be employed in ten seconds or less to give you control in situations where stress threatens to shut you down—whether you're a SWAT officer facing a gunman or a researcher like Audrey facing a conference room full of colleagues.

But first, let me discuss the stress response, because understanding it is the first step in learning how to manage it.

Stress and How It Affects You

Under extreme pressure the human body reacts in predictable ways. Everybody has his or her own definition of extreme pressure, of course. For some it's a FedEx package that fails to arrive, whereas for others the stock market has to crash before they'd feel truly stressed. But whatever it takes for us to feel really stressed, we *respond* to that feeling nearly the same.

The renowned sports psychologist Robert M. Nideffer, Ph.D., actually quantified that response in the mid-1970s. He postulated that no matter what the stressor—a mugger with a gun or a car that won't start, going for a job interview or facing a room of tough clients—his model consistently and accurately described the physiological, mental, and attentional reaction in his subjects.

The physical response was already well documented. In what's termed the fight or flight response, the hypothalamus, a golf-ball-sized organ nestled deep in your gray matter, releases two powerful hormones, epinephrine and norepinephrine. The effect of these hormones is to trigger a constellation of involuntary responses, including the release of adrenaline, another hormone, from the adrenal cortex. In seconds, that flood of adrenaline in the bloodstream speeds up your heart and breathing, effectively pumping blood into your extremities so you can fight or flee the stressor.

If the stressor were a mugger with a gun, you might owe your life to this involuntary response. On the other hand, if you're interviewing for a job or preparing to address the board of directors, you might wish you could run.

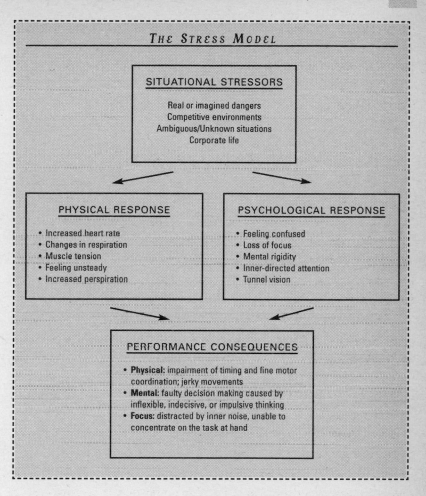

THE STRESS MODEL

SITUATIONAL STRESSORS

Real or imagined dangers
Competitive environments
Ambiguous/Unknown situations
Corporate life

PHYSICAL RESPONSE

• Increased heart rate
• Changes in respiration
• Muscle tension
• Feeling unsteady
• Increased perspiration

PSYCHOLOGICAL RESPONSE

• Feeling confused
• Loss of focus
• Mental rigidity
• Inner-directed attention
• Tunnel vision

PERFORMANCE CONSEQUENCES

• **Physical:** impairment of timing and fine motor coordination; jerky movements
• **Mental:** faulty decision making caused by inflexible, indecisive, or impulsive thinking
• **Focus:** distracted by inner noise, unable to concentrate on the task at hand

Problem is, when all that energy and adrenaline have no physical outlet, they wreak havoc. Extremities like your hands and knees start to shake from the backup. Muscles tense, including your laryngeal muscles, so that you feel like you're choking, and you can't speak. Your heart's pounding so hard it hurts. You're breathing so fast and shallowly that you're practically hyperventilating. Your mouth is dry but your hands are clammy, and the flush rising to your face is so intense it feels like your head will explode. And those butterflies in your stomach, that sensation bordering on nausea? That's truly in your stomach, not in your head, the result of stomach acid flooding in while blood rushes out to your limbs.

Then the mind reacts. Specifically, the left hemisphere of your brain goes into overdrive, noting and disapproving of all the physical reactions beyond its control. *You're screwed,* the left brain insists. *I've analyzed the situation, and it doesn't look good for you. In fact, it's hopeless.*

This voice of doom won't shut up—if anything, the commentary just gets more insistent. *Just look at yourself!* the voice hammers. *You're a wreck! You've been given this chance to show your stuff, and you're just going to make a fool of yourself! People can see you shaking—you, the Responsible Heavyweight around here. Your cover is blown! They're going to know you've been winging it all along. They're going to see you for the impostor, the fraud that you really are. Your career is over. Certainly your days are numbered. And if you lose this job, then what? How are you going to make your mortgage payment? What'll your friends and family think?*

What if? rants the left brain, on and on, faster and faster. It doesn't see possibilities; it sees only failure or perfection. It doesn't allow for mistakes; it demands you follow instructions to the letter. *There's no time!* it screams, scattering your thoughts further. You can't think; you can't make a decision; you can't tell what's a priority and what's irrelevant. You're like the woman who seizes the mail on her way out of her burning home, instead of saving her family's photo albums. Panic has made you stupid.

Stress can also make you lose touch with external reality, so focused are you on your own meltdown and its consequences. Your attention turns inward, to your pounding heart, your aching throat muscles, the imaginary details of your doomsday scenario. Your hearing gets annoyingly selective, filtering out all but the noise of jets overhead, or chair legs scraping around the conference table, or a distant phone no one seems to pick up. You can't seem to take in what's going on around you; your vision narrows down to a tunnel, so that you can see only the immediate threat, real or imagined—whether it's the barrel of the mugger's gun or the whiteboard you're supposed to be using in your presentation.

Now comes the worst part. Maybe you open your mouth, and a squeaky, high-pitched voice comes out. Maybe you attempt to write on that whiteboard, and sure enough, your hand is so palsied no one can read what you've written. It's just as your left brain said: You're making a fool of yourself, and your life is over unless by some miracle you get it together in the next minute.

So panic washes over you anew, and more adrenaline floods your overloaded system, and if there was any hope of getting back on track, it's gone now. Your mental reaction effectively perpetuates the physical one in a vicious feedback loop. You stumble in your delivery; your mind leaps on that mistake, obsessing over it, predicting more; and your body gets another shot of adrenaline, so indeed, trembling with excess energy, you stumble some more.

And still, postmortem, the left brain natters away at you. *What did I tell you? You're not up to this. You probably never will be.*

This is the typical human response. But there are those who respond to stress with all the energy but none of the negatives. These are the people who win Olympic gold medals; who hit solid high notes in solo performances at the Met; who race around a track at 160 mph and beat out thirty competitors; who galvanize an audience with their oratory skills; who make multimillion-dollar decisions without flinching. For these people, stress can be the catalyst to optimal performance.

You can be one of them. You can take that nervous energy and channel it, direct it, harness it into a force that will coax out your best performance under the most hideous pressure. You can use it to focus your concentration, silence the sabotaging voice of the left brain, and tap into the talent and training your right brain is ready to unleash. It's a matter of getting control of your stress response so that it's not involuntary. It's a matter of learning how to get your energy, in seconds, at the level at which you perform optimally.

It's a matter of learning how to center.

Controlling Your Energy

Centering is the seven-step process Nideffer came up with after studying aikido, one of the most mental of the martial arts, in Japan. What fascinated him were the feats the aikido masters could perform with seemingly no brute force. Their movements were more like ballet than fighting. And yet the power of those movements was like nothing he'd ever witnessed—a dazzling display of mind over matter, focus over force.

Nideffer, a former college athlete, got his black belt in aikido. He came back to the States and got his doctorate in psychology. And the pieces started coming together: not just the stress model but the solution to the involuntary stress response. What he created, in centering, was a tool that, unlike meditation, could be employed by anyone, anywhere, in any position, under any circumstances, to immediate effect. With practice, scatterbrained thinking could be transformed into quiet concentration in less than ten seconds.

The effectiveness of the technique was in helping people shift their thinking from the left brain, which is inclined to analyze, criticize, and distract with instructions, to the right brain, that quiet place where we allow our instinct, training, and muscle memory to take over and let us perform rather than obsess about the quality of the performance.

I learned centering from Nideffer himself as his student at United States International University in San Diego, where I was working on my doctorate in 1982. He'd been a competitive diver, I was a diver. He was a world-renowned sports psychologist, I was working my way toward that goal. He was my professor, but in the course of writing my dissertation he became my mentor, because I took his centering technique and put it on clinical trial.

I was particularly interested in seeing how effective it was in modulating energy *down*—down from that incapacitating energy level known as panic, because panic, rather than resignation, is what most people experience under stress. I wanted to test it under extreme conditions, more extreme than most people would ever encounter. I wanted to see if the members of the San Diego SWAT team could per-form any better if they employed Nideffer's centering technique to fo-cus themselves before firing. With the consent of their lieutenant, I got half his team in a room and told them I was going to improve their shooting skills without ever having them pick up a weapon.

The cops themselves were initially very skeptical. It helped that I was a West Point grad and a former Green Beret. It helped that many of them had taken a course I taught at National University, also in San Diego, on terrorism and counterterrorism. It probably helped that a lot of them were former athletes, because it wasn't a big cognitive leap for them to view shooting as an athletic event that I was qualified to coach, as a sports psychologist. And while centering wasn't exactly tough-guy stuff, it wasn't lying on the floor for twenty minutes sharing inner fantasies. They also liked the fact that this technique was based on a martial art.

But I can remember how they sat in their chairs listening to me, arms folded, jaws set.

I walked them through the seven steps, as I'm going to walk you in just a minute. I watched them close their eyes, and I noticed their breathing. They seemed to be following my instructions, but I had no real way of knowing. I couldn't read their faces. No one spoke but me. When we were done, I handed out sheets I'd printed out with the seven steps, and urged them to practice. Two weeks later I did a fol-low-up session to reinforce their centering practice.

Soon after that, we ran the test. The test was a move-and-shoot drill conducted in what's called a Hogan's Alley—a Hollywood-studio-like setting constructed especially for police training, with dirt embankments behind the structure to catch the live ammunition. There was a street lined with building fronts, and behind the fronts were rooms where pairs of targets sprang up from the floor randomly. Each officer would run, one at a time, about a hundred yards before stopping in front of a building to load his weapon. The bullets were real. Then he'd enter the building that his instructor, who was by his side, directed him into, not knowing what was going to happen in-side—what "people" would pop up where and when. "Hostiles"—

bad guys with guns—were purposely paired with "innocents"—women holding groceries or babies.

The officers were to move at top speed, we told them, because they were being timed. For every hostile they shot they'd earn ten points, but for every innocent they hit, they'd lose ten points. They were being graded on both judgment and accuracy.

What made the test so compelling were statistics the public would be appalled to learn about how badly cops shoot under stress. My research indicated that, under the extreme conditions Hogan's Alley simulated, an officer might empty his gun before he got off one shot that hit the right target. (In the Amadou Diallo case in New York City, forty-one shots were fired by four cops at an unarmed, unshielded man, and only nineteen hit him.) That's terrible performance. In fact, one of the Hogan's Alley instructors had been shot because an officer got so addled he swung around and fired at point-blank range before he recognized the instructor as an innocent.

In terms of judgment—differentiating between the innocent women and the armed killers—the group to whom I'd given just two lessons in centering performed significantly better than their colleagues. The ones who employed the technique while loading their weapon in the seconds before they entered the building scored, on average, +37.75. A perfect score would have been +50 (all hostiles killed, no innocents), whereas a completely failing score would have been -50 (all innocents gunned down, but no hostiles). In comparison, the SWAT guys whom I hadn't trained scored, on average, +21.94.

Those results made my dissertation headline news. The wires ran the story, and I got a call from the FBI SWAT team in Quantico, Virginia, asking me if I would come train their agents. The Chula Vista police wanted me to teach their 911 operators how not to seize up during emergency calls. The San Diego police SWAT team commander called me back to train the other half of his team. And just a few months later, when a madman opened fire in a McDonald's in nearby San Ysidro, it was a sniper from this SWAT team who took out the gunman on the first shot.

HOW TO CENTER DOWN

Centering works, as I've said, by getting you to shift from left-brain to right-brain thinking—from words and instructions to images and sensations, from negative, paralyzing analysis to positive action. It's not rocket science; absolutely anyone can learn it. With practice, anyone can make this shift in a matter of seconds. While the technique can be used to modulate your energy either up or down—to whatever level you perform optimally—I'm going to restrict this lesson to *centering down*. Later, in Chapter Five, we'll talk about *centering up*.

Start by learning how to do proper abdominal breathing. Lie on the floor with one hand on your chest and the other on your stomach. Breathing slowly in through the nose, let the air fill up your belly so it rises—without your chest moving. Breathe out through your mouth, consciously keeping the exhale slow and even.

When you've mastered this, practice breathing abdominally in a sitting position, with your hands relaxed in your lap. Once you're able to do this, stand with your feet shoulder width apart, arms hanging relaxed at your sides. What you're looking for is a position where you're balanced and able to relax. It may help to hang your head or rest your chin on your chest.

Before learning to center, it's important to have mastered this breathing technique in all three positions: lying, sitting, and standing. Then,

Step 1: Form your clear intention. What is it you intend to do once you've centered? Determine exactly what you want to do as soon as you're done centering. Focus on one action, one purpose, one goal. Right now, since you're a beginner, your goal is to learn how to center, so you might say, "I'm going to learn how to center." But under other circumstances—if you were trying to sell somebody on your product or service, for instance—then your intention would be, "I'm going to convince this buyer to sign a contract with me." If you were headed into a job interview, then your intention would be to convince the interviewer you are the most qualified person for the job. If you're hitting a tee shot, then you'd say, "I'm going to drive this ball down the center of the fairway."

Use assertive language, as in "I intend" or "I'm going to" rather than the more tentative "I hope to." Don't waffle; don't muddy your intention with qualifiers. "I'm going to confront my boss about giving me a raise" is much better than "I'm going to ask my boss if he thinks I might be due for a salary increase."

And above all, don't use "don't." For reasons having to do with the way your subconscious receives instruction, this word does not communicate a clear intention. "Don't bomb" or "don't miss" is absolutely to be avoided, because what your subconscious hears is "bomb" or "miss."

Step 2: Pick a focal point. Find something to fix your gaze upon that's some distance away and below eye level. Right now, that might be a piece of paper on the desktop, or your briefcase by the door of your office. If you're sitting in traffic, it might be the taillight of the car in front of you. This focal point is where you're going to direct the enormous energy that accompanies stressful performances or adverse circumstances. When the time comes, you're going to hurl your excess energy at this focal point, much as a pitcher unleashes a hard ball at the catcher's mitt. It's easier to throw a ball fast and accurately to a target that's lower than eye level—hence the pitcher's mound. And it's easier to release your ball of energy downward too—hence the importance of a low focal point. It happens that the more upward your eyes drift, the more actively you engage your left brain. And that's what we're trying to avoid.

Step 3: Breathe mindfully. Close your eyes. Breathe abdominally, as I just described. Feel your belly expand fully before your chest moves. Pay attention to your breathing. Inhale through your nose, breathe out through your mouth, slowly, regulating the exhalation so that it's even. Do this breathing mindfully until that's pretty much all you're focused on. Don't worry if this takes a while.

You're likely to have a lot of extraneous thoughts rush in, including "Is this really effective?" or "Am I doing this right?"

Just suspend disbelief. You're practicing. The more you practice, the easier it will get to focus on your breathing past any other thoughts.

Step 4: Release tension. Muscle tension is one of the most crippling side effects of stress. It's incredibly prone to the bad feedback syndrome: The more tense you are, the more poorly you perform, and the more tense you become.

With your eyes closed, and continuing to breathe in through your nose and out through your mouth, scan for muscle tension. The hot spots are usually the shoulders, neck, jaw and face, and forearms and hands—but do a top-to-toe inventory, paying special attention to your upper body. Check one area per inhale. When you find tension, consciously relax that muscle on the exhale. Imagine you are literally venting the stress. It may take anywhere from three to ten breaths, at this point, to release whatever tension you've been stockpiling.

Step 5: Find your center. Everyone has a center of gravity. Anyone involved in an activity requiring balance—dancers, rock climbers, gymnasts, surfers, skiers, skateboarders—understands, at some level, that his or her performance stems from this center of gravity. The rest of us, however, may need some help locating it and getting a feel for it.

It's about two inches lower than your navel and two inches below the surface—what some people would describe as the floor of their gut. Take a moment to see if you can feel it, inside. It may help to put your hand there.

If you can't feel it, it's important to try this exercise: Stand with your feet shoulder width apart, so you're "grounded," hands hanging by your sides, knees slightly flexed. Close your eyes. Now move your hips as though you're keeping a hula hoop going around your hips. Picture the hula hoop staying up; with each rotation, picture it getting smaller. Move your hips in tighter and tighter rotations, until the hoop is about the circumference of a bracelet, inside your gut. What's keeping it going can be described as your center, the point about an inch below this imaginary hoop.

Now try to remember how that feels, so you can locate it sitting down. In a chair, you might need to rotate your hips again to find it. Sense the contact of your "seat bones" on the chair; imagine you are trying to adhere every bit of your lower back to the seat back. Sink into it. Release those muscles so you get more contact. You should feel rooted to the chair and, by extension, the floor.

The whole idea behind finding your center is to feel rooted, grounded, stabilized—and in control of your energy. Stress has a tendency to lift you up and away from this place of balance and control. When you're excited or nervous, your shoulders climb, your breathing gets high in your chest, and your belly feels knotted. But notice what else: You literally stand on your tiptoes. How balanced are you then? I could knock you over with a frown.

Don't worry if you can't find your exact center. Its location is not so important as directing your attention and energy downward, until it hits bottom, or until you feel you're at ground zero or "on base." Breathe mindfully at least five times once you're there.

Because you're focusing on a sensation, your mind is quieting. That's because processing sensory input is a right-brain function, one that effectively shuts up the annoying chatter your left brain feels obliged to supply. Concentration is like a still pond: Left-brain thoughts are like gravel spraying it, whereas right-brain sensations smooth it out. Finding your center helps you begin to transition from left to right hemispheres by preempting your thoughts with literally a "gut" feeling.

Step 6: Repeat your process cue. You've gotten the left brain quiet; now it's time to call the right brain into action, into whatever you know how to do if only you could relax enough to do it.

You trigger action with something called a *process cue*. Process cues can be words or phrases that summon an image, sound, or sensation (nonemotional feelings). Better yet, they're the actual images, sounds, or sensations you associate with performing well, because the best process cues require no left-brain thought.

If you're about to deliver a speech or presentation, that cue might be the sound of the first couple words—not the actual words so much as the sound of your speaking voice: enthusiastic, inflective, loud, assured. Hear the sound of that voice, or flash before your mind's eye an image of you galvanizing an audience. If you've actually delivered a speech that went so well that people congratulated you, and you felt on top of the world—say, at the '98 convention—then your process cue might be just that: " '98 convention." A news anchorwoman I worked with made up an acronym for her process cue—"catch swamp bugs"—out of all the traits she thought were important to her delivery. (BUGS stood for *believable, unflappable, grace, sincerity*.) When I was playing golf with the faculty at Golf Digest Schools, my process cue, before swinging, was either "smooth" or "good tempo." It locked me into a feeling, a feeling my right brain remembered from every nice shot I'd ever made when I was relaxed. And it often served me well. I'll never forget the morning after an all-night party with the pros and clients, I found myself teeing off with Tom Watson. I was hungover (my golf game wasn't that great to begin with), and I was terrified I wouldn't even make contact with the ball. But I said, "smooth, good tempo," and my reputation was spared.

One of the most effective process cues is a piece of music. Like no other medium, music can put you in a right-brain mind-set, a mood, a place, a time. Snippets from songs—like the theme from *Chariots of Fire* or *Rocky*—don't just conjure the movie: You hear the refrain, and you feel caught up in the whole emotional spirit of the picture. Greg Louganis, possibly the world's greatest diver, cued himself for a dive by hearing, in his head, opening refrains from shows like *The Wiz*. "Hearing" a few bars of thrilling music can psych you up, just as hearing the opening of Pachelbel's Canon can slow you down.

In short, a good process cue, used at the right moment, can be
the mental equivalent of throwing a switch. Off with the left-brain
chatter, on with the muscle memory the right brain is retrieving
from your subconscious storehouse.

Step 7: Direct your energy. Remember that focal point I had
you choose many breaths ago? It's time now to open your eyes and
hurl your energy at it like a hard ball.

Your energy emanates from your center, so gather it up there
and let it travel up, up, through your torso, up through your neck,
and out your eyes like X-ray vision. Or to go back to our pitching
metaphor, you're going to do the mental equivalent of a pitcher's
windup, summoning every bit of power in your body and concentrating it into one directed motion that will release that power
aimed at your target. The pitcher has a clear intention—a slider, a
curveball, a change-up—and that's what he's about to realize. You,
too, are releasing your energy with a clear intention in mind, one
that you are about to make a reality.

At the moment of release, you are literally letting go. You're going to trust in your ability, instinct, and experience. And guess
what? They won't let you down.

Centering takes practice. I recommend three to seven times a
day. You may immediately feel results; alternatively, your left brain
may have exerted dominance for so long it's unwilling to be un-
seated so easily. You can monitor your progress over the course of
three weeks in the Energy Plan I have included as Appendix B in
the back of the book.

You can also take advantage of stressful opportunities throughout your day to practice. You probably won't be able to close your
eyes, or sit down, or be by yourself, but that's the point: Stress
rarely overwhelms you when you're seated and undistracted. Every
spike in blood pressure is an occasion to practice. Are you due for
a confrontation? Expecting a-tough sell? Need to ask for money, or
funds, or an investment? Is your computer malfunctioning? Are

you stuck in rush-hour traffic? Is there bad news you've got to deliver or digest? Center!

Within a week you should feel better armed for whatever your day throws at you. Sometimes, just knowing you have a strategy to revert to, knowing you have this technique to focus on, accomplishes the very thing you're after: the calm that comes from feeling you're in control, rather than at the mercy of your physiological reflexes.

Centering will get easier and faster. You may find yourself relaxing tension in a breath or two. You may find you can feel your center without even searching. You might even take a few mindful breaths and cue your right brain. Everyone arrives at their own condensation. Give it time to arise through practice, and you won't have to give the technique much time when you really need it to kick in fast.

Putting It into Practice

When Audrey and I met, she told me she wasn't interested in exploring her childhood fears and reasons for her particular performance anxiety. She had a problem; if she didn't fix it, she was going to have an even bigger problem; and she wanted me to give her a solution, "even though," she admitted, "I really doubt there's anything you can do."

Audrey's big problem was in getting this explosion of nervous energy under control to the point where it could work *for* her, instead of against her. "You're like a car going eighty-five miles an hour on a one-way street," I said. I taught her to center. We spent a lot of time on the relaxation aspect. I wanted her to feel like she was racing across the Mojave Desert instead of on the one-way street. I urged her to practice.

A week went by, and nothing changed for her. Another week went by; still no change.

Was she practicing? "I haven't really had the time," she hedged. "It seems . . . silly."

But one Saturday afternoon when she was home all by herself, Audrey started to work at it. She spent a long time just breathing and trying to focus on her breath. She practiced mindful breathing until she could no longer hear that pestering voice that said, *This is silly.* She spent even more time scanning her body for tension. She relaxed her shoulders, which felt like they were strung with steel suspension cables. She worked on her neck muscles. She went down each arm, right to the palm, to the tips of each finger.

"I could even feel tension in the arches of my feet," she admitted. "But by the time I was done, you couldn't have given me a massage that felt any better. I went from a hundred miles an hour to zero."

The weird thing, Audrey reported, was that after she opened her eyes, she got up, went to the piano, and played stuff she hadn't looked at in ten years. It just poured out of her. She didn't worry about mistakes. She made very few.

Audrey started practicing centering at every possible opportunity— on the train, at her desk, in the bathroom, and of course, before going into a meeting. She'd spend two or three minutes if she could; after a week, she got it down to a minute.

These days, Audrey actually looks forward to making presentations. Centering's taught her how to get to that matter-of-fact place her involuntary nervousness used to deny her. "I've stopped attaching life-and-death consequences to what I have to say and how I say it," she explains. "I remind myself I just wish to contribute."

But most important, the technique has made Audrey feel better. She realized she hadn't relaxed—truly relaxed—for four or five years.

"I'd been wound tight as a coil," she added, "and I'd felt really *bad*, physically, all that time. I didn't have to feel that way. I could choose not to. I had some control, after all."

Centering Down

When you start practicing centering, it should take you between fifteen and forty-five breaths, which will take thirty seconds to three minutes. As with any learned skill, your ability to center will improve with correct practice and repetition. Start out by practicing centering three to seven times a day. If you use it as part of your daily routine, you will soon notice positive effects. Eventually, you will be able to center in one to three breaths—that is, ten seconds or less.

When you start practicing, though, the goal is not to see how fast you can do it, but to accomplish the task of each step in the centering process. Make sure that you first form a clear intention and pick a focus point, then start proper breathing before scanning your key muscles for tension. Take as many breaths as you need to get relatively relaxed and find your center before repeating your process cue and switching to your right brain. Then reconnect with your center and allow the energy to rise up from there, through the center of your body, up and out to your focus point. Trust your talent and training so you can smile and courageously go for it!

You will soon experience that centering will take you from a suboptimal state of tight muscles and overthinking to one that is much more suited for optimal performance. The more you become familiar with that place, the easier and quicker it will be to get there. By the end of a week's practice, you should be centering much better and starting to realize significant results.

SUMMARY

Panic is our typical response to overwhelming stress. Panic impairs our fine motor coordination and sense of timing; confuses us so we can't prioritize information or make good decisions; and destroys our ability to focus on the task at hand. Yet our response to stress need not be involuntary. Panic or nervousness is simply energy, and energy is something we can control. **High energy can be either harnessed** to bring out your optimal performance **or modulated** to the level at which you perform your best. Learning to control one's energy, at will, is a matter of learning **how to center.** This chapter focuses on **centering down—bringing energy down to a more functional level.** Its seven steps are:

1. Form a clear intention.
2. Pick a focal point.
3. Breathe mindfully.
4. Release tension.
5. Find your center.
6. Repeat your process cue.
7. Direct your energy.

With practice this technique can be performed in less than ten seconds. Mastery is critical because centering is the prerequisite for many of the techniques and exercises described in the following chapters.

Turn to Appendix B for your own personal Energy Plan.

CHAPTER THREE

Perspective: How to Improve Your Outlook

*The thing always happens that you really believe in; and
the belief in a thing makes it happen.*

—FRANK LLOYD WRIGHT

The first thing Jeff Hull said to me, when we met in Los Gatos, California, in the mid-nineties, was that he needed "an attitude adjustment."

Things hadn't been going well, he explained. The mortgage sales business he'd launched a couple years before had unraveled. He'd been engaged to be married; in less than a year, that seven-year relationship had fallen apart. A month ago he'd been rear-ended on the freeway.

"Not that I'm suicidal or anything," he hastened to add, "but everything I do now I just feel that so many bad things have happened, it's going to turn out bad, too, even if it's going well."

Jeff was at a loss to help himself. He'd been very goal-oriented; his competitive model was one he'd taken from sports, where "you set a goal, work your butt off, and get to the next level." It had worked when he played college football. It wasn't working now. He couldn't understand it.

"What are you saying to yourself?" I asked him.

"If I set a goal, and I don't achieve it, then I'm a failure," he responded.

"Were you ever in a game, playing football, where you thought about the next play as you wanted it to happen and then, before your very eyes, this outcome you'd envisioned took place?"

Jeff nodded.

"Did you ever conclude," I continued, "that because you thought about it, and saw it in your mind's eye, that's why it happened?"

Jeff had never given it much thought.

But over the next six months, he would give it a lot of thought. Because little by little, his life turned around. And all we did was adjust his attitude.

What Is Perspective?

What if I said your expectations shape reality?

Or that your outlook affects the outcome of your actions?

Or that the odds are affected by your attitude toward them?

You'd probably say I was nuts.

Reality, you might insist, is shaped by a set of forces beyond anyone's control. The world turns on its own axis, oblivious to our personal wishes. So many factors affecting us are out of our control.

You're entitled to your opinion, of course. But if that's your outlook—if you really believe that the things you say to yourself, plus the images you hold in your head, have little to do with how events play out—it may explain why success has eluded you.

In this chapter I'm going to help you improve your *perspective*, because it is so formative an influence on your reality. How your prospects look from your point of view is how they really are and what you believe about yourself absolutely determines who you will become.

Perspective has three components:

* Your *self-confidence*—how you feel about yourself going into a situation
* Your *self-talk*—the things you say to yourself, about yourself
* Your *expectancy*—the things you envision happening, the outcomes you expect, the pictures you see in your mind's eye

If any of these components are not positive—if you're not feeling confident or your head is filled with self-flagellating criticism or doomsday videos—then we must work on changing them. We'll examine the role of self-confidence—how it affects you and how you can affect it with right actions. Then I'll lay out for you the phenomenon of negative self-talk—the way the left brain interferes with performance, the way the subconscious executes what the left brain says, and the way we sabotage ourselves with criticism. To change your talk from negative to positive, I'll show you how to monitor it and then reprogram it with affirmations. Finally, we'll tackle the topic of negative expectancy, the mental horror flicks most of us play when we can least afford to glimpse disaster ahead or revisit past defeat. These, too, can be banished by substituting what I call highlight films, which are clips taken from past performances that went well. If none are available, then you can create positive new footage with a technique called mental rehearsal.

Your self-confidence, self-talk, and expectancy are at this very moment writing your future. So let's get started.

The Power of Self-Confidence

The universe is governed by factors and forces that operate independently of you. Yet your perception of the universe changes depending on how you feel about yourself at any given moment. In effect, then, your feelings affect the universe—or at least, *your* universe. It looks different and behaves differently depending on your state of mind. So if you're brimming with confidence, your corner of the universe tends to behave more positively.

Let's say the corner of the universe you're focused on is the stock market, a world governed by a variety of forces and random events—everything from unemployment figures to an outbreak of mad cow disease—beyond our control.

Yet the phenomenon every Wall Streeter can attest to is that high investor confidence does, to a remarkable degree, create a market unaffected by such fundamentals as price-to-earnings ratios or dividends. Confident they could not lose in the tech sector, investors flocked in 1999 to get in on many stocks that had no revenues. Even in the face of rising interest rates and a roller-coaster NASDAQ, their mind-set remained unshakably positive. And to a remarkable extent the market continued to reward them for their confidence.

In short, investors who collectively *believe* they cannot fail do not. What they think is what they get. (Look at it this way: Should investor confidence suddenly evaporate, does anyone doubt the effect on the stock market?)

Now let's look at your individual confidence. No doubt it goes up and down, depending on what experiences befall you—experiences over which you have no control. Maybe you have the ill fortune to submit a proposal to your boss the morning after he learns his wife has filed for divorce. Or maybe you draw the 5:00 P.M. time slot to deliver your presentation on particle physics to a grant committee. Or maybe you lose a near-certain deal because of a missed phone message. Stuff happens. Your confidence can suffer from these external hits.

Yet look at the wins you've racked up, and consider how your confidence and outlook may have figured in them. Fact is, when you've been feeling flush with success—when your judgment has been dead-on, when your instincts have served you well, when your grasp of the material has helped you persuade even hostile audiences—you're so oblivious to those external factors on which you've pinned failure in the past, they no longer figure in the equation. When you're brimming with self-assurance, those externals prove totally irrelevant. You have robbed them of their power to affect the outcome you expected and deserved.

Confidence has given you control over "reality." What you expect is what you get.

Muhammad Ali is most famously quoted for having said, "I am the greatest," but what's interesting is that he came out with that statement long before history proved him correct ("I said that even before I knew I was," Ali insists). The most successful competitors—whether in business or in sports—continue to tilt the odds in their favor simply by believing they can. They consistently manage to interpret external reality in a positive way, one that puts events and outcomes within their control. Their expectations are reflexively positive: They expect things to work out; they expect that when things don't, they'll have the tools to adapt or correct the situation; and they expect, in the end, to meet their goals. Hence the wins keep coming their way. And with each win, their confidence grows larger, affirming their positive outlook and ensuring it doesn't falter.

Confidence is like a pile of poker chips: The more you have, the more likely you'll play like a winner . . . and the more likely you'll *be* a winner. A lack of confidence doesn't preclude success, any more than a glut of confidence ensures an optimal outcome. Yet few would disagree that the more you have, the better.

STOCKPILE SMALL SUCCESSES

How do you build confidence? Two ways. The first is rather obvious: You need to pile up successes, however small. That means avoiding playing long shots, at least at first. For example:

* If you're feeling beaten up by the markets, now's not the time to liquidate your life insurance to buy the latest biotech com-

pany. Instead, pick stocks with small but consistent gains. Or get out of the stock market entirely; ply your skills in a game where the odds are overwhelmingly favorable until you get your sea legs back.

* If you're starting out as a sales rep with a new company, don't go knocking on CEOs' doors first; go with people you know, or people you've done business with before.

* If you're trying to get published, don't start out by sending your manuscript to the editor of the *New Yorker*. Better to feel out local publications for their editorial needs and send your work where it's actually welcomed—and where it stands a much better chance of getting published.

TAKING RIGHT ACTIONS

The second way to build self-confidence is advice your high school basketball coach probably gave you, but it's worth repeating: Focus on the fundamentals. Do the little things you know you should do but have maybe gotten lazy about. An artist knows she should sketch to warm up; a sprinter knows to stretch before racing; a soprano knows to warm up her voice to ensure she's able to hit the high notes. If you're a speechmaker, you know that no matter how good you are or have been, you still have to practice it beforehand, ideally in front of some people.

These are what I call *right actions*. They require that you park your ego and go back to the sort of basics you thought you were way past having to review. They can certainly shore up your confidence.

Platform diver Michelle Mitchell won silver medals in the 1984 and 1988 Olympic Games. During one national championship, Michelle performed a back one-and-a-half with three and a half twists—an incredibly demanding dive. She came out too early, however, and saw the platform instead of the pool, and lost her bearings. She hit the water on her side, curled in the fetal position. It was so bad that every news station in the country replayed the video of it in their "Agony of Defeat" sports footage for the day.

While the dive didn't injure Michelle physically, it freaked her out. Getting lost in a dive, losing all visual reference, is a diver's worst nightmare. Michelle couldn't stop replaying her nightmare. It was seriously eroding her trust in her ability. Her confidence, which was usually bulletproof, was so low that it was endangering her.

So we worked on her fundamentals. I made sure she did all the right things—all the little technical things divers learn, like getting a strong takeoff. She practiced that over and over, first in easy dives and then in progressively more difficult ones. We started on the side of the pool and worked up to the ten-meter platform. She racked up dozens of technically sound dives. Good muscle memory etched itself over bad. Her confidence gradually returned. Eventually, the nightmare dive no longer had the power to undermine her. She got her best dive back.

Right actions changed Michelle's perspective. After one disastrous blow to her confidence, she thought she couldn't do the dive, and indeed, she couldn't. Only a series of right actions could persuade her otherwise, even though her ability was there all along.

The Power of Self-Talk

What do you say to yourself when you're under pressure? Is it to do something right—or not do something wrong?

Maybe you don't know. Maybe you've never even thought about it. But it's time to tune in, because what you say to yourself, and the way you say it, will determine how you perform under pressure.

In my class at Juilliard, I have my students demonstrate this to themselves with a very simple exercise. Each of them is to choose between one of two statements:

I am weak.

I am strong.

Silently, they're to repeat to themselves the statement of their choice while holding out their arms at shoulder height. Another student presses down on their arms. How successfully they resist the downward pressure, they find, depends on what they've been telling themselves. The "strong" ones are strong; the "weak" ones are more often than not the ones who cannot keep their arms up.

Many more rigorously scientific studies have proved this correlation. What accounts for it is the mechanism of the mind. Whatever words issue from the left brain, whatever images arise from the right brain, all take root in the subconscious, which hasn't the analytical capability to pass any judgments on what it receives. It doesn't filter out anything; that would be out of its job description. It can't distinguish a joke from a serious directive. It can't distinguish reality from what's been merely imagined. Without questioning the data it receives, the subconscious takes everything the conscious mind dumps on it and makes it happen. The left brain talks; the subconscious follows through. The right brain visualizes; the subconscious executes the vision.

It's not just that the subconscious acts as a data bank. The repetitive, cumulative effect of both the left brain's shower of words and the right brain's stream of imagery is what makes the subconscious so formidable a mechanism. A word or picture doesn't get implanted once. It gets hammered in, over and over, day after day, week after week, until your subconscious responds like a robot. Chances are, you have no idea how profoundly your words and mental videos are affecting your subconscious; you're not conscious of the mechanism, because you see no correlation between what happens and what you've been thinking. But the correlation exists nonetheless. The corporate execs who commit millions of dollars to television advertising budgets do so because they know just how effective this mechanism is. Consider how automatically you reach for certain brands—the Diet Pepsi, the DiGiorno frozen pizza, the Tide detergent. Television programmed your subconscious, without you even knowing it. Your hand unconsciously executes the command it was given while you were zoning out in front of the tube.

The subconscious works this way regardless of the content of the input. It cannot discern, and does not discern, between good notions and bad. What you program it to do is up to you. If you load it with negative advice or directives, it dwells on the negative and makes happen exactly what you dread or fear. If you're sarcastic or facetious, if you joke to yourself or to your doubles partner on the tennis court, "Watch out! This serve could wind up over the fence!," the subconscious will execute the command and the ball will indeed head out of bounds. The subconscious has no sense of humor.

Nor does it understand the word "don't." If you've ever tried to drive a golf ball past a major hazard, like a lake, you know this to be true. Your left brain may have said, "Don't hit it into the water," but the only part of that instruction your subconscious hears is "hit it into the water." And the next thing you know, your ball's in the lake. Most of us routinely admonish ourselves. "Don't screw up," we murmur, or "Don't bomb" or "Better not blow this." But that's not the way to word a directive to the subconscious unless we want the worst to happen.

I worked with a world-class tennis player, in her twenties at the time, whose game was beginning to suffer from the overinvolvement of her father. During a Grand Slam tournament, he was on her case about her fiancé, whom he disapproved of, and she lost a big match. Afterward, at the top of the stairs in the stadium, disgusted with herself for losing to a lesser player, and feeling bleak about her future, she said to herself, "Don't fall and break your wrist."

She fell. And not only did she break her wrist, she broke the navicular bone, one of the most difficult bones in the body to heal. It proved to be a pivotal point in her career.

Most of the time, we're not even aware we're talking to ourselves. That's the whole problem: We're constantly sowing our subconscious with frightful weeds that will choke out any produce we hope to cultivate, but either we don't realize we're doing this or we don't believe self-talk to be as powerful as it is. Even what passes for humor—"I'd never miss a putt that short" or "I'm gonna go down in flames"—uttered before some kind of test or performance has the power to destroy, so I urge my clients not to jest. The subconscious has no sense of humor; it hears, and it obeys.

Negative self-talk is a bad habit. It can be changed—but like most habits, half the battle is becoming mindful of it enough to pounce on it.

Think back to your most recent not-so-wonderful performance. Say you gave your marketing pitch to a prospective client, and she didn't go for it. Can you reconstruct what was going through your head right before making the pitch?

If you've been giving a number of these pitches with a high rate of failure, I'll bet I can guess.

Something psychologists call *state-dependent learning* tends to lock us into unhelpful mind-sets and destructive self-talk. Simply said, we tend to respond to a situation in whatever way a similar situation made us respond in the past. So if trying to close a deal with a client reminds you of your last unsuccessful attempt to ask your boss for a raise, then you're likely to have a lousy outlook on the deal's prospects, because you can't help but apply to this client the negative thoughts from your last encounter with your boss.

More broadly stated, in the face of hardship, we recall previous hardships. If the way we handled those previous difficulties proved unsuccessful, then, just when we need a shot of confidence most, we're infused with the rhetoric of failure. So when it would be most beneficial for you to recall a stunning marketing success, you instead play the tape in your head when you got turned down cold.

Jeff Hull was prone to just this kind of debilitating feedback. Soon after we began working on his outlook, he joined a Silicon Valley start-up which sold the hubs and switchers computers use to communicate with each other. As is typical of any start-up business, the first months were pretty hand-to-mouth. Since Jeff was in charge of the books and the sales, he had a better idea than anybody of the company's short-term health and long-term prospects. But he had trouble evaluating the data objectively because the situation so reminded him of his first and unsuccessful entrepreneurial attempt. "So many times I'd come home and think we were going down in flames because I saw all the same signs I'd seen in my mortgage sales business," Jeff admitted. "*The writing's on the wall,* I'd say to myself. *We're going down in flames.* I'd sit there and wallow in it until I couldn't even move, I was so full of fear and dread."

It's easy to feel victimized by this reflex; by definition, reflexes are something you can't seem to help.

But you can. You can fend off the negative outlook a tough situation triggers. You can change the tape from one of the past to one of your choosing. All it takes is raising your consciousness. Be aware of your self-talk, and you can begin to turn things around.

MONITORING YOUR SELF-TALK

Some of my clients wear a wristwatch that beeps; I have them set it to beep every few hours throughout the day. Whenever their watch goes off, they're to stop what they're doing and write down exactly what they were thinking, in the mind's exact words.

Alternatively, let the ring of the telephone serve as your prompt. What was going through your head between the time you heard it ring and the moment you picked it up? Put it down on paper. Try to pin down the exact language.

I realize it's quite difficult to capture these thoughts verbatim— after all, we are not in the habit of thinking about our thinking. But it doesn't really matter: Just trying to get our thoughts on paper is in itself making you conscious of what's normally outside of your awareness. This writing exercise, repeated throughout the day, is enough to get you much better attuned to the conversation that's been going on in your left brain. You're going to be on your guard for left-brain sabotage, and that's the first step to being able to switch off the lousy tape.

To catch your left brain in the act, carry a little notepad around with you for a day or two. Tell yourself you're going to write down every negative word or diatribe; keep the notepad handy or visible so you remember your assignment. Stop yourself mid-tirade and write down what was said to your subconscious.

No matter how silly or predictable this exercise feels, I strongly urge you to do it. The act of writing—of formulating thoughts into words, of nailing down vague notions with specific language—brings what was reflexive and out of your control into the purview of the conscious mind. It's like taking your most awful, repugnant sins and confessing them, either to a priest or to a counselor. Getting them into the light of day, getting them heard, immediately diminishes their horror, and their power over you.

So it's not enough to say, "I get the idea," and then turn this page. If you don't nail down those swirling thoughts, they stay out of your reach and your ability to change them. Putting the damaging script before your eyes limits it to something you can certainly manage or overcome.

PERSONIFYING THE VOICE

Once it's down on paper, look at it and consider this: Would you *ever* say such things to a colleague or friend?

A news broadcaster I worked with, Bonnie Anderson of CNN, was having an awful time going live before the camera thanks to her self-talk, so I asked her to pick someone in her crew whom she felt she mentored, someone who looked up to her. She chose her producer. I told her to imagine trading places with him: to imagine him going before the camera live and to picture herself as the producer communicating with him via his earpiece. If she were talking into his ear, what would be her tone? What would she say to help him bring out his best performance on camera? Would she dare abuse him with what she'd been in the habit of saying to herself? Would she ever, in a million years, say stuff like, "You dumb shit! You idiot!"?

That helped Bonnie a lot with her self-talk.

I also had her give a name to this abusive voice who whispered in her ear. She called it Nasty Nellie. By personifying this voice and making it someone other than herself, Bonnie could "tell" Nellie to shut up. Even better, Bonnie started to find Nellie a pathetic character, someone whose opinion she couldn't possibly value. Just thinking about her name would make Bonnie laugh. Nellie didn't have a chance after that.

REPROGRAMMING SELF-TALK

One of the opera singers I counseled came to me with a fairly common fear. She was terrified of missing her high notes. Ninety-nine times out of one hundred performances, she hadn't experienced any difficulty. But one of those times, when she'd been in a foreign city and was struggling to overcome a cold, she opened her mouth on stage and the wrong note came out. Ever since then, she had doubted her ability. Every time she needed to hit that high note it triggered an instant recall, not of the ninety-nine successes, but of the one failure. Her career had taken a downward spiral since that fateful performance.

We worked on her confidence in a number of ways. I got her to record and monitor just what self-damning words ripped through her mind prior to performing. And it wasn't long before she was able to write them out rather accurately. She'd become so aware, she said, that whenever that left-brain buzz saw started in with "Remember what happened in Berlin?," she'd say dismissively, "Yeah, yeah, yeah." Like she was hearing her mom say, "If you don't pick up your room, there'll be no going out tonight!" Or she'd cut the lecture short with an "Oh, shut up."

She learned to consciously stop the tape that automatically

kicked in whenever she had a cold (*You won't be able to sing your best when you're feeling this bad*) or had to hit a high note on stage (*Don't miss it*).

The next step was to change the tape. Rewrite it. Rerecord it.

For every negative comment she captured on paper, I had her recast it into a positive command. For instance:

Don't miss it became *Nail it.*

You won't be able . . . became *I know I can do this.*

I've missed it before became *I've hit it ninety-nine times out of a hundred.*

It's very important to remember how the subconscious receives information as you rewrite your self-talk. Use positive directives. Treat your subconscious as a young child, one you adore, one you wouldn't dream of hurting, one who you know will respond much better if you use a positive tone and specific, concrete language. Young children don't understand what you mean when you snap, "Behave!," for example, but if instead you say, "I'd like you to stay in your seat and remember to say please and thank you at dinner," you're likely to get compliance. Same with the subconscious: Be specific, clearly state what you want rather than what you don't want, and be affirming.

REPROGRAMMING WITH AFFIRMATIONS

Dierdre, a client of mine who's an Episcopalian priest, suffered a chronic lack of confidence as she delivered her sermon. We worked on her centering technique, with particular emphasis on relaxing and breathing, and I had her write out her self-talk, which she could recall pretty easily, since she always told herself the same thing: *I can't do this. I just can't. It's always been this way, it always will be this way, and I can't do it. I won't get anywhere. What is the matter with these people that they put up with me, that they don't see?*

To deal with this negative commentary, Dierdre took my advice and ran with it. She spent forty-five minutes or so a day filling up pages with everything positive she could think of. "I'd write about what was going well, or what I'd learned, or what I was pleased with about myself or my life—in bullet form," she explained. "It was very affirming. And it was real clear to me that on those mornings, even though I couldn't spare the time, things went much, much better."

WRITING AFFIRMATIONS

Listing affirmations can be very powerful, but most people have great difficulty committing to paper what they think went well, because it sounds so corny, so Pollyanna. Men in particular resist putting into print emotional breakthroughs like, "I did a better job expressing my love for my kids."

There are guidelines for writing down affirmations which can make the process easier:

* The most powerful affirmations begin with the words "I am." Those two little words and what follows them have great impact on the subconscious.
* Take care to phrase the statement positively, and do it in a way that is true today and will be even more true tomorrow: "I am focusing better and better," or "My mind is becoming more and more quiet," or "I am responding better and better to . . ." These affirmations don't overstate the facts; they predict them.
* Once you've got the hang of writing your affirmations, the final steps are to say them silently to yourself and then out loud. Affirmations then become exactly the antidote to negative self-talk, because (1) they're positive, (2) they're voiced mindfully, not surreptitiously, and (3) they go right into your subconscious mind.

Bonnie Anderson took a slightly different approach to her affirmations. She itemized ideal traits, those she wanted to exhibit during live broadcasts. Here's a sampling from the list she came up with:

confident
authoritative
poised
warm
believable

She recast these into affirmations. They became:

I am more and more confident during live broadcasts.
I come across more authoritatively with each broadcast.
I am increasingly poised before the camera.
I am warm and conversational.
I am even more believable live than I am on tape.

As I mentioned in Chapter Two, Bonnie took her list and worked out an acronym that comprised all of these traits: "Catch swamp bugs." It became her process cue, the words that, during the centering process, would trigger the subconscious to kick in and deliver the goods—in this case, all those attributes. It worked for Bonnie, not because in saying it she mentally cataloged the trait that each letter represented, but because it made her laugh—and mirth is an invaluable weapon against the self-talk harpies. Laughter acts just like the switch on the tape player that cuts off the tape and ejects it.

What happens when you do these exercises can be self-revelatory . . . and unpleasant. Once you lift the veil, you might be truly offended by what a load of crap and abuse you've been heaping on yourself. Keep a sense of humor. Or just say, in the midst of the melodrama you're hearing, "*That's* interesting." Don't get caught up in it. Get some distance. Laughter can give you that perspective.

Change What You Tell Yourself

- Monitor your self-talk. Learn what things you're telling yourself by checking in on your left brain periodically throughout the day or after stressful events, especially those that didn't go well. Write them down verbatim if you can. Pay special attention to the things you'd never say to a friend or colleague.
- Tell the critic to shut up, or say, "Yeah, yeah, yeah," dismissively.
- Rewrite the internal dialogue. Start changing "don't" statements to "do" statements. Use positive, concrete language.
- Write a list of affirmations or keep a journal in which you note only the positive—what you did right, what you've learned, what you feel good about, what you're grateful for, how you've grown.
- Give this exercise some time. With practice the left brain gets quieter.

A Picture's Worth a Thousand Words

What you say in terms of self-talk is incredibly influential in terms of programming self-confidence either up or down. But what happens under stress is not limited to the left brain's barrage of critical words or negative thoughts; the right brain, in the space of an instant, churns out pictures that can be equally damaging. And because every picture is worth a thousand words, these mental movies pack a thousand times the punch of the words the left brain spews.

Under stress, not just any movie comes to mind. Our right brain dredges from our subconscious films about stressful situations we actually starred in, taken from our past. Depending on how we handled our role, and depending on the outcome of that situation, we're looking either at hero films or at horror flicks.

It could be either. But for reasons peculiar to the human psyche, we're inclined to watch mostly the horror flicks. Or maybe it's just the state-dependent learning phenomenon: When we're scared, all we can remember are those past circumstances that similarly scared us. All it takes is one sensory cue—a particular sound, a certain smell, a kind of lighting—to remind us of a past crisis and start playing the tragic movie of it in our mind's eye.

Like the words that assail us under pressure, these images, these mental movies, are so reflexive, we're barely aware we're watching them. But you need to become aware, because even more so than negative self-talk, doomsday videos have the power to undo you at the worst possible moment.

HIGHLIGHT FILMS

There are two ways to blot out harmful images. One is to take actual footage from real life, footage in which you, the star, are performing beautifully. Earlier in this chapter I mentioned how Michelle Mitchell overcame her fear of losing herself in a dive. She went back to working on her fundamentals and slowly replaced the image the TV cameras had given her with one of her own making, taken from real experience, in which she did the dive, again and again, the right way.

But reprogramming the mind's movie library doesn't demand you go out and get the experience, as Michelle did, in order to get new footage for your mind to dwell on. You can create "highlight films," using your imagination, that double for real experience, because the subconscious does not differentiate between what you imagine vividly and what you experience. Sometimes there is no way to go out and get the positive, reaffirming experience your image bank needs in order to squelch out the doomsday flicks; sometimes your only choice is to imagine the experience before it actually happens. It's a technique called *mental rehearsal*. And it works because the subconscious is terribly gullible.

MENTAL REHEARSAL

Steve Shelton, a race car driver, was coming around a curve in the St. Petersburg Grand Prix when he lost his brakes. He had a millisecond to make an awful choice: crash into a concrete wall or plow into a crowd of onlookers. He chose the wall. Remarkably, although he got pretty banged up, he only broke his arm; the next day, with his arm in a cast, he was ready to drive. However, like Michelle Mitchell, Steve wasn't ready mentally. He couldn't stop playing the movie where every time he rounded this curve, he lost his brakes. Never mind that the chances of that happening again were very small; never mind that he had handled the crisis as optimally as he could. Fear isn't an emotion that responds to reason.

Practicing driving through that section of the course until he proved to himself that his brakes wouldn't fail would no doubt have eventually cured Steve of his fear. But he wasn't going to get that opportunity. Grand Prix courses are city streets. Drivers never get as much time as they'd like to learn the course.

So before he got in his car to compete that morning, Steve rehearsed the turn in his mind. He visualized himself going through it effortlessly, over and over, as he would need to during the race. He practiced the thing he feared until he got it right—but he practiced it in his mind, with his imagination. He experienced, mentally, how he would hold the wheel, what shift sequence he would use, when he would clutch, accelerate, and apply the brakes. He saw, in his mind's eye, the car responding beautifully.

Lap after lap he negotiated that turn well. Even with a broken arm, he finished second. His second-place finish gave him enough points to ultimately win the series championship that year.

We did a lot more mental rehearsing, because it was frequently Steve's only way to practice a course before competing on it. Sometimes we'd walk the course or drive it at regular speeds and tape it with a video camera. Back in his trailer, Steve would view the tape and then practice "seeing" it with his eyes closed. And when he got it down visually, he practiced driving it—mentally marking where to accelerate, downshift, pass, brake, etc. This was the most important step, because in mentally racing, Steve was no longer thinking: He was *experiencing* the action, etching into his subconscious exactly what he needed to do when the time came. His imaginary drive was so vivid, so visceral, his subconscious could not possibly discern between it and the real thing.

Mental rehearsal takes a certain amount of discipline. In spite of all the studies showing it's extremely effective, in spite of all the fatigue and danger it spares you, in spite of the fact it saves a lot of time and energy—people tend to skip it. Americans, that is, tend to skip it, perhaps because we lack the cultural history that affirms its value. Unlike the Russians and East Germans and Japanese, we don't have the religious or secular teachings that show how mental rehearsal helped leaders vanquish their enemies and beat impossible odds. I can only urge you to give it a try. And I can show you how profound a contribution it has made to the success of individuals we all admire.

One of the greatest masters of mental rehearsal I ever met was Greg Louganis, the Olympic diver. Greg calmed his pre-competition jitters the night before by putting on music and mentally going through all his dives, putting himself through every takeoff, dive, and entry until his muscles twitched and clenched in response. Sometimes he watched himself, mentally, from the vantage point of a judge below. If he saw a mistake, he had himself climb out of the water, get up on the platform again, and do it over until his muscles recorded just how it felt to do the dive correctly.

He used the technique even to learn new dives. It helped him cut down the practice time needed to get them right, and it even lessened the amount of physical pain he wound up enduring.

"In my training, I'd make the correction my coach was asking for before I got on the board," he explained to me. "Some athletes have to figure it out physically, but I didn't want to go through that kind of pain. And I found I didn't have to—I didn't wipe out as much as the other guys did."

Greg learned mental rehearsal when he was only three years old. Before a performance, his dance instructor had him lie on the floor and, while the music played, go through the motions in his mind.

Guidelines for Rehearsing Mentally

- Start by centering (see page 51 if you need a refresher on technique). Make sure you do a whole-body check for any hidden tension. Breathe mindfully until it's the only bodily noise you're conscious of. Select a visual reference point that relates to the beginning of your performance— for example, the door of the conference room in which you're about to give a brief talk.
- Hear in your head the first several lines of your speech. See yourself looking excited and confident as you walk in. Feel yourself making good gestures as you stand at the head of the conference table. Hear yourself sounding assured, speaking with inflection and passion.
- If you make a mistake, don't beat yourself up. This is only rehearsal. Mistakes are why you rehearse: to experience them and find a way to handle them. Start over. Give it another shot. Slow down the action until you get it right. You can always play it again faster, and then eventually at regular speed. The important thing is that you experience it right, that you do it correctly, so that your subconscious records the experience for reference later. You don't stand a chance of pulling off a great performance if you've never allowed your subconscious to experience what that looks and feels like.
- For long performances, don't do more than twenty minutes at a time. In one session, just rehearse the beginning. In the next, start where you left off. In anywhere from three to five sessions, you want to have imagined your performance totally from beginning to end without exhausting yourself.

Be creative and have fun. Keep track of your sessions in the perspective log at the end of this book. With just a little bit of practice, you'll start to reap rewarding results.

That way he could practice, she explained, without getting really tired and worn-out. Greg had no problem doing what she asked. Three-year-olds, he notes, don't exactly suffer from a lack of imagination; in fact, they mix up the real with the imagined all the time.

He's relied on mental rehearsal throughout his career, which has included a one-man stage show in New York and innumerable speaking engagements. To make the rehearsing process more fun, and to relax him into the right-brain state of mind where he can hear or see himself performing, he listens to music—often inspirational stuff from sound tracks ("If You Believe," from *The Wiz,* is one he's gone back to many times). He also makes sure he gets a look at the place where he's to act or speak, so that he can plug into his rehearsal all the actual visuals, plus a few that he imagines (like an audience in the seats).

"I always assumed everybody did this," Greg told me, surprised that I was so interested in the details.

Think what a world it would be if everybody did.

The Power of Perspective

What you feel about yourself and your prospects, what you tell yourself, and what you expect are what determines outcome. Program into your subconscious right actions, an encouraging word, an inspiring image, and watch reality unfold as you previewed it. To make it even easier, turn to Appendix C for a step-by-step guide to improving your own perspective in just three weeks.

It's that simple.

But only if you're aware that it works this way.

Jeff Hull sees the handwriting on the wall rather differently these days. In the first year of business, the company in which he's now a part owner did $6 million in sales, as opposed to the $3 million that was projected; the next year, they did $20 million; this past year, sales topped $50 million.

There are times when Jeff wonders if it isn't all too good to be true. The business could tank as quickly as it grew, he thinks—and then he catches himself.

"I have the tools to adjust that attitude now," he adds. "I no longer think, *What if we go out of business?* but rather, *Well, if that ever happens, I know I'll meet the people that will help me continue down another path.*

"It's not that I'm making things go my way," explains Jeff. "It's more that I perceive them going my way. The way you look at a situation is the way you make it work for you."

SUMMARY

The most successful competitors tilt the odds in their favor simply by believing they can. They consistently manage to interpret external reality in a positive way, one that puts events and outcomes within their control. They expect things to work out; they believe that no matter what the outcome, they'll have the tools to adapt or make the best of the situation. In short, they expect, ultimately, to triumph—and so they do.

This chapter explores how you can acquire this enormously powerful mind-set. There are three tactics:

1. Improving your self-confidence by:

- Accumulating small wins
- Taking right actions

2. Making your self-talk positive by:

- Monitoring it
- Talking back to the left-brain critic
- Reprogramming the directives the subconscious receives
- Replacing negative commentary with affirming, positive statements

3. Replacing doomsday videos with:

- Highlight films drawn from past experience
- Highlight films vividly imagined through mental rehearsal

Turn to Appendix C at the back of the book for a detailed, personalized Perspective Plan.

CHAPTER FOUR

Courage: How to Become a Risk Taker

Whatever you do, you need courage . . . To map out a course of action and follow it to an end requires some of the same courage which a soldier needs.

—RALPH WALDO EMERSON

Every year it was the same event: Hospital administrators from all over the country assembled for a two-day conference paneled by a dozen industry leaders.

And every year Jake*, fifty-two, experienced the same mortal dread: He would have to introduce each of the panel members, because it was at his invitation that they had come to speak.

Each of them required about a two-minute review of their credentials and accomplishments. He'd have to discuss, briefly, what set them apart from the pack, what kind of institution they ran, what particular problem they had addressed. He'd need to throw out a few career highlights and maybe mention how he'd come to know them.

Not a big deal.

Yet for Jake, a lifelong stutterer, making introductions was like burning at the stake.

"It's a chronic performance," he told me. "You don't get up once and get it over with. And names aren't like words. You get hung up on a word, you can always find another that will serve just as well, but if you can't get out someone's name, you're stuck: There are no replacements."

The fear of introducing a well-spoken panelist whom 350 people had paid nine hundred dollars each to hear and getting hopelessly stymied on the first syllable of the guy's name—this fear was so debilitating, Jake admitted to me, that if one of the candidates he was considering as a speaker had a name that gave him trouble, he might reject him, no matter how qualified he was.

"That's when I figured I needed to get some help on this," he said. "Blowing down a couple of martinis wasn't going to be enough to get me through it."

What Is Courage?

Courage is not the absence of fear. Courage is doing the thing you fear. Or as General Omar Bradley put it, "Bravery is the capacity to perform properly even when you're scared half to death."

It's an act of volition: There is always the option of giving in to the fear, finding a way out of taking any risk. There is always the option of doing nothing.

Success isn't won, however, by those who won't risk it. Success isn't awarded to those who sit on their hands, cling to the status quo, do the safe thing, "wait and see," or otherwise assume a defensive, passive stance. The *ability to risk* is the ability to seize the initiative. Whatever's worth having is worth taking a risk to get. You can't steal second with your foot on first.

Success demands taking action when the results are not guaranteed.

Success demands you have the *ability to risk defeat*—that you acknowledge the possibility of failure, and its consequences, and act anyway. You don't allow yourself to dwell on fear; you go for it. That's confronting fear of defeat. That's courageous action. On the other hand, people who score low in this ability are so concerned with the possibility of failure, they can't act at all. Fear of failure immobilizes them. They can't cope with failure as an outcome. So they do nothing.

When fear of failure immobilizes, defeat is almost certain. Or, as the saying goes, He who hesitates is lost.

One of the few pieces of military history I remember from my West Point days underscores this point. It was the siege of Petersburg, seat of the Confederates, during the Civil War. Union troops attacked what was called the Dimmock Line, a ten-mile wall of earth with placements for 55 artillery batteries. They attacked with nearly 6,000 troops. Only 125 Confederates, mostly men either too young or too old to be in the army, met their advance. But the two Union generals grossly overestimated what they were up against. After only a day's fighting, they withdrew. Unsure how to proceed, they decided to wait for reinforcements.

That gave the South just enough time to amass its own army of 18,000 at the Dimmock Line. And so began the ten-month siege of Petersburg, which ultimately resulted in over 70,000 casualties—all because of two generals who gave in to fear of failure at the moment they might have been victorious.

Fear is different from self-doubt. Doubts are thoughts, as we explored in the last chapter; fears are emotions, emotions so primitive they operate outside cognitive function. Fear is irrational. It's based not on reality but our interpretation of it, an interpretation skewed by false evidence we conjure in our imaginations. And once we allow a flicker of terror, a fearful image to enter our consciousness, it spreads like wildfire. One brief glance at your calendar, showing an upcoming presentation, and you can be engulfed with adrenaline and catastrophic scenarios. Not that you're going to die giving a talk, but you may feel as if you will. Fear isn't mindful of the facts.

Fear colors every human experience. It's the human condition. We're afraid of forgetting our airline tickets, of being late, of missing the boat. We're afraid of being yelled at, or of having to yell at someone else. We're afraid for our children; we're afraid of our boss. We're afraid of failing. We're afraid, even, of what success may bring.

We'll be discussing fear of success in this chapter, because it's not as uncommon as you might think. The *ability to risk success* is the ability to embrace success with all its consequences, whatever they may be. Getting what you want usually involves some undesirable consequences. If you fear those consequences, or just fear what you cannot anticipate, then you will score low in this factor. Scoring high, on the other hand, means that you're willing to risk whatever upheavals or changes success may bring, because you believe you can and will handle anything.

Most of the exercises in this chapter are designed to counter fear of humiliation. Even race car drivers fear finishing in last place more than they fear crashing and burning. No one wants to look the fool. (Why else do so many people insist that public speaking is what they fear more than death?) We're deathly afraid of being perceived losers, people who just don't measure up and never will. Then there's the Big One: *What if I go all out, do my best—and it's not enough? What will people think?*

Know this, however: Whatever your fear, you can conquer it. Action—not lying on the therapist's couch—is what overcomes it. You need to get moving. You need to embark on a training regimen. Courage is like a muscle: Fear atrophies it; action flexes it, works it, gradually strengthens it. Your workouts should increase in difficulty and duration gradually, over a three-week period. The key is to start small and practice that small step over and over until it becomes second nature. Second nature needs to be well developed, because it's got to override your instinctive nature—the fear response. You can reprogram instinct. It takes extensive repetitive training.

In Ranger School we learned to rappel out of helicopters hovering at one hundred feet. We weren't superhumanly courageous; we were just rigorously trained. Because let me tell you, it goes against every instinct to jump into a barely controlled free fall. We learned first to rappel butt-first off boulders. We practiced the "L" position—bent at the waist, legs out straight, and feet against the cliff—over and over, because the overwhelming inclination is to cling to the rock with your entire body. We practiced on higher and higher cliffs. Only after we'd done dozens of rappels off the cliff were we ready for the helicopter.

Military training is effective because it's so repetitious: You do what you're trained to do. After a while, you don't even have to think. That prevents fear from having a moment to take root and dictate what you should do—which is good, because fear will propel you either to do the wrong thing or to do nothing at all.

If you're caught in an ambush in the jungle, fear will make you take note of where the fire is coming from and then turn and run like hell. It's a powerful instinct, but it's one that will get you shot in the back. As commandos we were taught, through repetition, how to face the fire and advance. Only by facing the source of fear and bearing down on it did we learn how to live to see another day.

This chapter, if you do the exercises, will get your courage muscle in shape to face the fire, whether it's giving a speech in front of several hundred hostile faces or committing hundreds of millions of investor dollars to a high-tech merger. You won't be rid of your fears, necessarily; but you will no longer be paralyzed by them. You will have come to trust yourself enough to act, to risk defeat, even in the face of fear.

Trusting yourself comes only from the experience of having done it before, so that's where we'll begin: examining your experiences for instances of risk taking that you may not have considered courageous or may simply not remember that way. You've doubtless been courageous. You do *have* the ability to risk; you just may not realize it. I'll help you prove it to yourself by helping you find lots of evidence of past courageous action. We'll use three tools: the Courage Journal, the Courage Log, and symbols of success. Then we'll do some assertiveness training, by way of flexing your newfound courage in small ways, to get the hang of it. Indulging your humor is one of these ways.

When you've gotten more assertive, you'll be strong enough to "act as if"—a strategy useful in helping you overcome your fears, whether they're from confronting failure or confronting success. And finally, I'll help you "go for it" by showing you how committed action always wins out over tentative gestures or passivity.

The Ability to Risk

As I've said, courage is an act of volition: It is what you choose to do. Knowing you have exercised choice instead of being swept along like a leaf is a big confidence booster. It's believing that you have no choice that breeds anxiety.

For years, my client Jake had chosen to chair this major conference, a choice that entailed interviewing prospective speakers and ultimately being a speaker himself on the day of the event. He could have chosen not to do the introductions; not to handpick the speakers; not to organize the conference. He could have chosen to get himself out of hospital administration altogether. All along, he had choice, and he chose to do the gutsy thing.

Only, he didn't see it this way. He didn't see his role in bringing himself to the very place he now dreaded. Being master of his fate had made him master of ceremonies. But instead of feeling self-confident, Jake suffered the anxiety of a man backed into a corner.

My goal with Jake was to change his perception of himself from someone desperate to muddle through to someone who consistently chose to do the courageous thing, from a victim who reacted to his fate to a victor who understood that he steered it. Simply by committing himself to the task of speaking, Jake had acted courageously. Many, many little acts of courage had conspired to bring him this far. If he could see that—if he could examine the past in a new light, where just not copping out counted as courage—then he'd be well on his way to seeing himself as having already conquered fear many times before.

From that remembrance of courage he could derive the self-confidence and strength he'd need to banish his particular bogeyman—the fear of stuttering.

When I started working with Jake, I was amazed to hear him describe himself as a stutterer, because, to the contrary, he was incredibly articulate. When I pointed that out, he nodded. "As a matter of fact," he said, smiling, "I'm often called in by the speakers I've hired to help craft and polish their speech!"

As long as he was talking one-on-one, or even in small groups, he explained, the stutter didn't rear itself. He'd long ago acquired the knack of substituting words the millisecond he got hung up on one. But always, in every public speaking situation, particularly when names were involved, Jake feared the stutter would come back to embarrass him. It was the reputational risk. He was afraid a stutter would show him to his peers and colleagues as someone flawed, someone other than the person they had come to respect and admire.

The fear was laid down in high school when, as president of the honor society, Jake had to make a presentation before the entire school. When he practiced his speech in front of five hundred empty seats, he was great. But during the actual event, he hit such a verbal wall he had to stop midspeech and retreat from the podium.

"That's the moment I go back to compulsively," he said, "even though I never stuttered like that again, because that's the moment I froze and retreated in absolute shame." (That's the irrational nature of fear, of course. It has no head for statistics. Probabilities mean nothing to it.)

The shame burned so hot that Jake refused to let others change his perception of the event. High school friends of his who ran into him at a coffee shop later said, "That was the greatest act of courage, to just get up there in the first place and give a speech." Jake dismissed them. He couldn't take them seriously.

But what if they were right? I asked him.

It was Jake's choice to perceive the speech as a moment of extreme

cowardice and failure. Therefore, it was equally his choice to stop perceiving it that way. He could just as easily perceive, as his friends had,
that merely agreeing to get up there was a supreme act of courage.

He could choose, that is, to transform the memory into one that
proved his mettle.

The task I set before him was to go through his memory well, fish-
ing for acts of courage that may have sunk to the bottom simply because he didn't record them as such, and drag them into the light for
reexamination. He was to document these past acts in a journal.

THE COURAGE JOURNAL

For the past twenty-five years, Jake had never given himself credit
for handling all the logistics of the conference: arranging hotel
rooms, booking conference facilities, hiring caterers and setting up
banquets, making travel arrangements for the speakers and contingency plans should any of them not show at the last minute. Interviewing speakers was only the half of it; picking up the phone and
interviewing complete strangers was another challenge, another
"chronic performance" Jake elected to undertake. Coming up with
ten of these—ten actions that took guts, that threw him into the
crucible of his fear—wasn't easy at first. Like most people, Jake kept
looking for heroic gestures—instances when he'd rescued someone
from a burning building or stopped a gunman. I had to remind him
he was looking for acts as simple as picking up the phone or turning down a speaker candidate.

With each one recalled, Jake was quicker to come up with the
next.

I had him write them down in his Courage Journal. Remembering them wasn't enough, I stressed. By writing them down he
was etching them into his mind, where they would be instantly ac-
cessible in a moment of crisis. Writing them down helped smother
the fearful fires he tended to fan reflexively. He recalled what ter-

ror or anxiety had gripped him before he'd committed to doing the courageous thing; I wanted him to see and remember what fears he'd gotten past. And I had him write down the outcome, because even if the outcome wasn't good—even if he screwed up or had to back away from the podium—it served to show that he had endured. He may have suffered, but he hadn't died. He'd gotten past it. He'd handled it.

That is the real basis for the Courage Journal. It serves as a reminder that, over and over, you have taken risks and handled the consequences, good or bad. In your own Courage Journal:

* Recall and record ten acts of courage, or ten things that took guts, or ten things that filled you with fear but you went ahead and did anyway.
* Record what you were afraid of, prior to undertaking these actions.
* Record how these actions panned out.

Knowing you have handled the worst is a formidable weapon against fear: It didn't kill you, it made you stronger. Without the journal to remind you, however, it's easy to forget how much you've handled. Writing helps you tap a source of power you forgot you had earned.

Jake's journal did more than just remind him he had endured. Revisiting the past, perceiving the risks he'd taken in everyday actions, Jake started to see how much *choice* he had exercised. Things hadn't just happened to him. He hadn't arrived at this point in his career arbitrarily. He hadn't, in fact, just "muddled through." Time and again he had chosen to act, to take risks, to not allow an incident from the past to hinder him from seizing control of his future. Every act that made him face his fear had contributed to his success, even when the outcome of those actions hadn't always been favorable.

COURAGE JOURNAL			
Event/Situation	Fear	Action You Took	Result
1			
2			
3			
4			
5			
6			
7			
8			
9			
10			

"Remembering those moments, and coming to understand what made me do the things I did, I started to think, *Gee—I deserve to be here. I've* earned *the right to be here,*" Jake said.

Later, after the conference, we spoke again. "It's amazing how little anxiety I felt," he said. "The conference seemed to just slide by this year. Even my wife said, 'You're so much calmer.'

"I don't know if I can reconstruct my state of mind during the event so I can borrow it back for next year," Jake mused. "But maybe I don't have to. Maybe it's enough that I did it."

As I hope I made clear in the previous chapter, perception is everything. It's not reality but how we interpret it that influences our actions and the results we garner from them. When we perceive in past events evidence of our courage, then we feel the confidence to take further risk. Our real potential begins at the edge of our comfort zone. When we push the envelope, when we test our limits, we grow in strength and advance our capabilities. That's how we move closer to our goals.

THE COURAGE LOG

The Courage Journal is very useful in terms of boosting confidence by raising your consciousness of past risks taken, past fears you handled. That's good, but it's not enough. It's just as important to raise your awareness of what brave actions you're taking now. It's important to keep, if only for a brief time (again, three weeks is about right), a day-to-day log of these actions. Too many of your accomplishments go completely unremarked, I can bet. They deserve applause or a slap on the back; they deserve acknowledgment.

Here's the idea: You keep track of actions you take every day that show spunk or initiative until you acquire the perception of yourself as a risk taker.

1. Develop your radar for opportunities to exercise your courage. You might have trouble perceiving any action in your day as "courageous"—the tendency is to look for heroic gestures worthy of front-page news. But keep an eye out for things you went ahead and did that would have been just as easy not to do. For instance:

- If you picked up the phone and scheduled a bunch of marketing calls, that deserves mention in your log. (Never mind if you made them out of fear your division was going to be dissolved if you didn't bring on a bunch of new clients. Remind yourself you had a choice, and you chose to do the spunky thing.)
- If you confronted a subordinate who's been slacking off, a confrontation you've been avoiding for some time, definitely write that down. (Even if you did it to suck up to your boss, you still might have chosen a more painless path.)
- If you took one tiny step toward setting yourself up in business—getting your marketing materials printed up, or looking into individual health care plans—put it down.

2. Write them in the log. See the sample Courage Log on page 97. Your goal is to write in the log no fewer than twenty-one of these, however seemingly inconsequential, whatever the actual consequence. Over a three-week period, that would be one per day—I bet you can find more than that once you get into it.

3. Give yourself permission to postpone action. It's what you do, not what you fail to do, that you want to put into your conscious brain. Don't write down what you chose not to do.

The Courage Log is like a bankbook in which you record all your deposits. The act of recording them makes you feel like you're getting richer and richer, even if the actual amounts deposited aren't that big. That's the whole idea: to feel richer. Because then you'll feel like you can afford to take a risk.

COURAGE LOG

21 days

Event/Situation	Fear	Action You Took	Result
1			
2			
3			
4			
5			
6			
7			
8			
9			
10			
11			
12			
13			
14			
15			
16			
17			
18			
19			
20			
21			

SURROUND YOURSELF WITH SYMBOLS

As inventories of personal courage, both the log and the journal make for inspirational reading material. But once you've completed them, all you really need to do is picture them in your mind's eye, or see them in your top drawer or in your briefcase, to be reminded of all that they represent. In other words, the sight of them is enough to tap into the deposits they hold. They are powerful symbols.

Symbols are a kind of mental shorthand. You see one—like the American flag—and your subconscious downloads an entire CD's worth of information. I'm of a mind you can't ever have too many symbols around you to remind you of your courage. If you've got palpable proof of having acted courageously, for heaven's sakes put it on display or have it somewhere you can sneak in a quick glance. Maybe you've got trophies from athletic events. Maybe you've got medals from military service. Maybe you've got photographs, or letters attesting to your having gone the extra mile. Most probably you've got diplomas. Don't underestimate their power! Think how many doctors' or lawyers' offices you've sat in, flanked by framed certificates: Aren't you impressed? That's why they're on the walls, these talismans of success, because anyone who looks at them, including the person who put them up there, is instantly made aware of the accomplishment they represent—the ordeals endured, the tests passed, the courage exercised, the honors earned. They serve as a process cue. One glance at that diploma from Harvard Law, and your fear—whether you're the alumnus or the client—instantly dissipates.

If you don't have this sort of physical evidence, I urge you to go out and get it. I worked with a professional musician who tackled a lot of fear and won herself an audition with the Los Angeles Philharmonic. I took her to the local army/navy store and encouraged her to pick out a medal—a Silver Star or Purple Heart. She laughed, but she did it, and put it on her instrument case. Every time she opened her case, there it was to remind her: She'd faced her fear, she'd chosen to act despite mortal dread, and she'd won. Even if she hadn't won, I would have pressed her to get the medal, because going for that audition took guts. Less than two weeks prior to the audition, she had lost an audition for a lesser orchestra in Florida. And a few months before that, she lost an audition in Minnesota—one in which she performed flawlessly except that she had learned the music wrong, by one phrase. That was the phrase she'd been working on when her mother died of cancer.

So find a symbol that will henceforth serve to remind you at a glance of what you took on—no matter what the outcome. You're rewarding yourself for trying. You're rewarding yourself for taking a risk, no matter to what degree you succeeded or failed. You get a lot of confidence points for trying.

And just a little confidence is all you need. Because like fear, confidence builds on itself. With a little confidence, you'll find the courage to take the action necessary to move you closer to your goals.

Taking Courageous Action

Now look at all the evidence that you're a risk taker: There's a journal full of past experiences; a day-to-day accounting of current ones; and perhaps a wall or desktop full of talismans symbolizing your courage.

Great. Bask in your newfound wealth. You're rich in confidence chips.

But don't just keep counting those chips. It's important to get them into play, to make them grow.

So let's look at a slightly tougher exercise, one that, with repetition, will definitely strengthen your resolve to act. Let's get you to be more assertive.

Assertiveness lies halfway between being passive and being too aggressive. It's acting out of honesty. It's being true to your beliefs to the point of acting on them. That may be confrontational.

Confrontation is something most people shrink from. They won't ask for what they want, or even what they deserve, because they fear being told no. Being rejected, or being ignored, is a form of failure. It's the worst kind, the kind wrapped in reputational risk: *How can I live with myself if I'm turned down! What will people think of me?*

But the irony here is that entertaining that fear is the surest way to fulfill it. Do you fear looking ineffectual? Guess what? You are ineffectual so long as you don't speak up or step in. Worried you're going to bomb? You're preparing for it every minute you spend obsessing on this possibility. Fear is like a magnet: What you fear is what you attract. The worst will happen not if you try and fail, but if don't try out of fear of failing.

I continue to work with George*, forty-one, a professor on the faculty of a prestigious law school. George is not a confrontational person; he's always prided himself on being a good mediator, someone who listens, who's polite, who can be counted on to mend fences, not rile the neighbors. Politically, this has been a valuable personality trait; it helped make him head of his department.

Yet for the past five years, he's been at a loss to correct a problem in his department that everyone is aware of: Certain faculty members are misgrading students purposely. The departmental infighting and competition among the professors for tenure are such, George explained, that some of them try and sabotage each other's reputation by penalizing each other's students in oral exams or other situations graded by jury.

George felt powerless to intervene. For a time he convinced himself confrontation wasn't the answer.

"But what that really meant was, I didn't feel I was capable of making a difference even if I did," he clarified. "I've always had confidence issues. Even when I think I know what the right thing to do is, I worry, *What will other people think?*"

We did some assertiveness training, starting with George's self-talk. *You're not persuasive,* it berated, or *You're not going to pull this off,* or *There are too many people, you're not going to succeed in changing their behavior.* His first confrontation was with himself. He was to tell this critical inner voice to shut up.

Then he was to call a meeting of the offending faculty members. I gave him a clear agenda to follow, one with almost universal application to confrontational situations. Here's how it goes:

HOW TO BE ASSERTIVE

1. **Define the situation as you see it.** State your observations in a factual manner. George said, "It's come to my attention that some faculty members are misgrading students. It appears they're taking out on the students the disputes they have with each other."

2. **In one sentence explain how this situation makes you feel.** This takes some forethought. You may feel angry, frustrated, powerless, taken advantage of, used, ready to scream, disappointed, full of knots, ready to pull the plug—but get it down to one clear statement. Don't accuse; say, "I feel . . ." Avoid making insinuations about others. Instead of, "You're being totally unprofessional," George said, "I feel it's unfair to the students."

3. **Finish by stating exactly what you would like to happen.** George planned ahead of time to say, "I would like you to resolve whatever issues you may have with each other face-to-face instead of having you work them out on the students."

George followed the script. He was really surprised at the results.

"Maybe because I went in there thinking, *I'm going to persuade them,* things went well," he said. "My main plan was to get these guys to talk to each other, because I think the misgrading was out of fear of each other. And they did talk; the two main offenders really vented their wrath. By the end of the meeting, they'd agreed to put this behind them. We'll see—it's too early to tell. But I feel I succeeded as a facilitator. I think by getting them to know each other better, I got them to listen to me."

But the real impact this had on George was in making him see it was within his power to make changes in his universe. No one would think less of him for trying, whereas they most surely would if he did nothing and allowed the situation to deteriorate further. He could afford to honor the good voice, the one that urged him not to settle for less.

"I've lived most of my life resigning myself to what I had, rather than believe I could make happen what I wanted," he told me. "Now I have this sense that I'm *creating* scenarios, not just surviving them."

Assertiveness doesn't have to take the form of confrontation. There is, however, a confrontational aspect to being assertive: You must reach out and engage others because only with their cooperation can you hope to achieve your goal. That's why it feels risky. They have the power to deny you. But here's what fear of being denied accomplishes: *denial!* If, out of fear of being turned down, you don't assert yourself, then you absolutely won't get what you want—an outcome identical to being told no. In other words, you have nothing to lose by trying—by reaching out to engage.

I worked with a lawyer whom we'll call Julie, an ambitious woman who had recently joined the mergers-and-acquisitions team at one of the biggest corporate law firms in Manhattan. Several months into her job, she sought me out because she felt that her boss, the head of this team, was toying with her, making her perform certain documentation reviews over and over.

"Right in front of everybody, he asks me to 'take another crack at' my reviews," she told me. "It's a terrible put-down. I'm starting to doubt my own ability."

It became clear, however, that her boss was generally quite satisfied with her work and her style. Julie was being given the heavyweight clients, the billion-dollar deals. Were it not for his nit-picking, she admitted, she could imagine herself on a partner track.

Julie gradually came to believe that her boss didn't intend to put her down; rather, he didn't understand that he came across that way in communicating what he wanted from her. What was needed was clarification—the sort that would come only from meeting with him one-on-one.

Julie was terrified. "How do I tell him he's got to handle me differently without risking looking weak?" she protested. "I can't afford to expose myself, to show vulnerability—even though every time he attacks me in meetings I feel like crying."

But I convinced her that it wasn't an option to continue on in her job as miserable as she was. She enjoyed her work, but the only way she could excel at her job was by restoring the pleasure she took in doing it. Confrontation of some sort was inevitable, so she might as well initiate it now, before her anger and resentment caused an outcome she might regret.

We scripted her lines, heeding the following ground rules:

1. She wasn't to go in and tell him he was wrong. That would be challenging his control, and she was his subordinate. Instead, she was to frame the problem as her own, while reminding him they would both benefit by its resolution. "It's important to us both that clients perceive me as authoritative, competent, and tough," she could say, "but when I'm criticized in a meeting, I have trouble appearing that way."

2. She was not to criticize, but rather, offer constructive solutions that honored their mutual goal—that is, helping the firm get the most out of her abilities and training. "I do my best work," she practiced saying, "when I feel I have your support and total confidence, especially in front of my colleagues."

3. It doesn't hurt to remind a superior that you respect his authority and do not challenge his control. Julie found she could say, "I'm honored to be on your team and to be entrusted with the re-

sponsibility you've given me. You've coached me so thoroughly that at this point, just a nod from you, just a glance, tells me exactly what you need me to do."

After rehearsing her lines with me, and sitting down with a few of her friends for practice, Julie met with her boss.

And to her total surprise and relief, it was a tremendous success.

"I opened by saying, 'I'd like to bring to your attention some issues you may not be aware of that are making it difficult for me to do my best work,'" she reported. "That got his attention. He helped me out by making guesses. Finally, I said, 'Are you aware that when you address me in the middle of a presentation, in front of five other men, I get very tense?'

"I think I made him feel he was more in control of what I contributed," Julie concluded. "He wasn't offended. He was flattered, because in a way, I was identifying him as my mentor. And he took my suggestion. Now, if the glance or gesture doesn't get through to me, he has his assistant set up a meeting for just the two of us, for a private chat."

As Julie found, people respond positively to forthright behavior because they don't have to do the work of second-guessing your agenda. (That, or they're so shocked at your candor and forthrightness they can't help but say yes.) Chances are, they'll reward you for your spunk, perhaps even in ways you don't anticipate. Not long after we spoke, Julie was rewarded with a raise that made her salary commensurate with the top-paid people in her elite profession.

USING YOUR HUMOR

Start by flexing your humor in nonpressure situations. Some guidelines:

* Look for the irony in everyday experience.
* Exaggerate things. "I've told you a million times, don't exaggerate!"

* Perceive double meanings in common expressions.
* Act the fool. Be silly.

This can be somewhat risky, depending on your audience. But taking a risk improves the odds of a favorable outcome. Let me tell you about John Golden, a champion amateur golfer I met when I was running a golf clinic in Vail, Colorado. Not long ago he succeeded in qualifying for the U.S. Senior Open. First day out on the course, after bogeying the first two holes, he found himself on the green with Jack Nicklaus and Graham Marsh. He waited for them to finish, and then he turned to Nicklaus and said, "Jack, I've bogeyed the first two, you parred. Do you mind if I press you here [to increase the wager]?"

It was supposed to be funny. Nicklaus eyed him with a steely look, said nothing, and continued playing.

After the first round, however, back in the clubhouse, he waved John over to join him and his wife for lunch—which John did.

The next day, on the fourteenth hole, John took another little risk. Nicklaus hit a big drive; John, who was up next, killed it too. As the ball was in the air, John blurted to it, in earshot of the entire gallery, "Get by him!" Get by him!" It didn't, but everybody laughed. And then Nicklaus retorted, "It's good to talk to your ball, John, but it's not going to listen to you." And everybody laughed again.

"For years I didn't play my best golf because I worried too much about what other people were thinking," John reflects. "I was afraid they'd think I was being cocky, acting like those guys on television. I struggled to find that middle ground, between being a blowhard and being modest.

"That day on the fourteenth hole, I got to pull Nicklaus's chain," John concluded. "I didn't beat him, but I was no longer intimidated by him; the minute he responded to my joke, the minute everybody laughed, I felt like we were equals. It was a little risk I took, but I was rewarded for it in so many ways."

Courage is asserting yourself—your thoughts, your feelings, your desires, or your humor—to other people. By doing so, you seize the upper hand, because, if only for a moment, you impose on them your agenda—what you want. You direct their thoughts. You affect their feelings. You *control* them.

And by doing so, you no longer have to worry, *What will they think?* You've just programmed their thoughts.

The best performers, the best athletes I've worked with, all recognize this, however instinctively. Make the audience laugh, and they're yours (why else do so many presentation experts advise you to open with a humorous anecdote?). By making his audience laugh, my friend John got himself in control of his nerves, and that put him in control of his game.

This is such an important way to boost confidence it deserves one more example. Greg Louganis, the world champion diver, is probably best remembered for winning the gold in '88 after hitting his head on the diving board. It was an awful moment for him, and for the audience, when it came time to get back up on the board and finish the competition with stitches in his scalp. The tension was so palpable you could hear the audience thinking collectively, *What if . . . ?*

So Greg did this incredible thing. He turned to the audience and all the television cameras, and he beat on his chest with his fist and made a face, like his heart was pounding out of his chest and he was terrified.

Everybody laughed. It diffused all the tension, not only in the audience but in Greg. He had altered their expectations for him. He was in control, that little gesture communicated, and there was nothing to worry about.

There wasn't.

Remember that. If you can laugh at your fear or use laughter to dissipate the fear you sense in others, you, too, will have nothing to worry about.

What to Do When You're Hit with a Zinger

Everybody's had the experience: that sudden, heart-slamming feeling that stops you cold in your tracks, or brings you to full alert at four in the morning. It accompanies the realizations I call zingers—the oh my God, I completely forgot to take this into account! thoughts that strike at random with deadly force. That one oversight instantaneously balloons into a vision of utter catastrophe.

Here's how to take the sting out of the zingers.

1. Say *out loud* exactly what it is you fear. Get it into the light of day so it looks less freaky and awful. Now tell yourself, *This is a perfectly normal way to feel.* You're taking control. You're addressing it.

2. Watch three "highlight films"—minute-long mental videos in which you star as the capable, competent person who, under even extreme pressure, does things right or saves the day. These can be taken from real life, from your past, or conjured from your imagination on the spot, because the right brain can't distinguish between what it has remembered and what it has imagined. (Why else do you think the catastrophe you imagine looks and feels so real?)

3. If you don't have time for these short clips, rely on your process cue— that word or image, sound or sensation, that reliably silences the critical commentary. The more it makes you smile or laugh, the better.

4. Alternatively—as Susan Jeffers says in her book *Feel the Fear and Do It Anyway*—just say to yourself, *I'll handle it.* An affirmation like that goes a long way toward short-circuiting the left brain and bypassing completely the paralysis that fear triggers.

You *will* handle it. You have already.

So: How's your courage muscle? Do you feel it bulking up? Are you finding more and more entries to put in your log?

The last courage-building exercise I want to discuss is definitely one you want to build up to. But it will without question transform you from a risk-averse person to a bold risk taker. You'll be Superman, with regard to confidence in your powers. You'll feel bulletproof. It's very simple in concept: You're going to *act as if* you're the Man of Steel.

HOW TO ACT AS IF

1. **Form a picture in your mind of whom you'd most like to be** in terms of confidence—a better salesperson, an entrepreneur, a deal-closer, a CEO—and get a feel for how this person looks, sounds, and behaves. If you were a professional actor, imagine this is the role you're auditioning for.

* What speech mannerisms might be characteristic?
* Which facial expressions?
* What's this person's body language?
* What clothes, accessories, uniform, or props do you associate with this character?

You'll need to think through ways to flesh out this person's character beyond what he or she might say.

2. **Get yourself the costume,** the uniform, the shoes, the cane, the hat, the briefcase, the hairdo, the Palm Pilot, the cell phone, the cologne, because clothes and accessories do make the man.

3. **Get into costume and get into character.** Practice, rehearse, experiment. The costume will help remind you of your job.

4. **Go out on stage.** When it's show time, leave yourself behind. You are an actor, and you have stepped into your role, so *act accordingly.*

When the show's over, you can of course revert to being you.

But don't be surprised if you become more like that character, or find it represents a side of yourself you never before knew or recognized.

Risking Defeat

For months I worked with a guy with courage issues whom we'll call Anthony.

Anthony, forty-four, worked in advertising. He managed the art department of one of the biggest firms in New York, and he'd been successful enough that after twenty-two years in the biz, he'd earned himself a four-day workweek—same salary, same perks, plus the freedom to nurture his artistic talent in a noncommercial way, which is what Anthony was pining to do.

He wanted to paint. He wanted to make his living as an artist. He wanted to be so good that he could get out of advertising altogether and support himself and his family without "selling out" any longer to the establishment. He knew he could paint; he knew he had the talent, the training, and the experience to be an artist. He just wasn't so sure he could make a living off of what he painted. He doubted he could pull off the sales end. He was terribly afraid of sales confrontations. If he asserted himself, if he asked gallery owners to represent him, he felt he was risking a highly personal form of rejection, because painting was self-expression. A "no" would mean "You're no good, I don't like your style, I don't think you're worthy of my esteem."

Or at least, that's what Anthony feared.

We worked on Anthony's self-confidence and courage in many ways. He filled out a Courage Journal. He kept a Courage Log. He practiced centering and mental rehearsal. Perhaps most helpful was his developing a "pre-event routine"—a series of little rituals he observed every time he walked into his studio, from playing with his paints on yesterday's palette to playing George Carlin tapes during his warm-up. The looser these warm-up exercises made him, the better he painted right off the bat (instead of burning through his entire three-day weekend trying to get down something good). The more fun he had in his studio, the more he enjoyed the actual painting, instead of beating himself up for not making any headway. The more he enjoyed himself, the better he painted—the more risks he took on canvas. And the better he painted, the more confident he became.

He got to feel so good about his work that he could shrug off even his own rejection. *So I didn't produce any works of art today,* he'd say to himself on days he painted poorly. *I took a risk. It didn't work out, but it wasn't pointless. I learned something from taking that risk, something I couldn't have learned any other way. And I had fun.*

Before Anthony made a single gallery call, he had so pushed his limits in painting that he felt he could afford to step outside his comfort zone with regard to selling. He felt he could afford to hear "no."

"They may not like my stuff, but they're not going to throw me out," he reasoned. "I have total confidence in the quality of my work. It's got integrity, and it's me. If one gallery doesn't like it, another one will."

Still, being a salesman invoked a totally different set of skills from those of an artist—or so at first Anthony believed. It felt as though being an artist and a huckster of art were mutually exclusive roles. How could he be one without sacrificing the other?

But that's where the "as if" technique proved of enormous value. Because in order to sell to galleries, Anthony didn't need to be a salesman. He needed only to *act as if* he were one—wear the clothes, talk the talk, act the part. At any time he could revert back to his shy, introverted self. If anything, the sales cover gave him some much-needed armor: If a gallery owner said no, it was the tough sales guy who took the hit, not criticism-sensitive Anthony.

The idea was liberating. Anthony felt free to exaggerate. He imagined his sales persona as someone brash and eccentric, forthright and fun—"a cross between Picasso and a guy I knew in high school." He got himself new clothes a la Lyle Lovett; he trimmed his beard into a goatee; he let his hair go rakish.

The final touch was a scarf—the signature artist's scarf. It wasn't just a prop or costume touch, though; it served as a symbol and a process cue. "Just feeling it around my neck acted as a reminder, like a rabbit's foot, of what my character needed to be," he explained. "My role was to be positive. Affirming. Hugely confident."

Anthony began with galleries he knew in SoHo. Acting the part live didn't turn out to be all that hard. "I strode in like Picasso," he recounted, "pushed my glasses up on my head, and stroked my goatee. I was loud, I was colorful. I even got the owners involved in my presentation, holding canvases while I trotted out others. One woman who knew me actually said, 'I like the new . . . !' She couldn't even fill in the blank. It was like I had a whole new personality."

Acting turned out to be easy, Anthony added, because he'd had plenty of practice. "As my wife pointed out, I've been acting for years. I put on this whole act at work every day because I hated what I was doing."

Anthony went into each gallery intent on one goal: He wanted to be given a show based on his most recent work. The salesman he played was so successful, however, he got offered more shows than he could handle.

"I've had to turn things down!" he marveled to me. "I walked into one gallery, one I didn't know, and in *one afternoon* got myself bought and established!"

More came out of it. Anthony won a month's sabbatical as an artist in residence at an out-of-state college. The local press interviewed him and ran a feature on his work; more calls started coming in, more galleries expressed interest.

Last I spoke to Anthony, he was living the bohemian life on campus while collecting full salary from his advertising firm, which wholly supported his new venture. He was freed from job, wife, kids, and his daily grind for a month of painting. He couldn't believe how his dream had taken shape.

"You can't fail if you think you're great," he reflected. "And if you don't feel that kind of confidence yet, then I'd say, 'Fake it till you make it.'"

The Ability to Risk Success

Fear of failure, of rejection, of bombing—these are the fears we're best acquainted with. But some individuals sabotage their own struggle to succeed, often without being aware they are, simply by fearing what success might bring. They're not ready to handle certain consequences of winning. And even a flicker of worry about those consequences can be enough to ensure they don't bring them about by winning.

In her book *Champions Are Raised, Not Born,* Olympic swimmer Summer Sanders tells how she missed qualifying for the '88 Olympics because of one tiny moment of fear—fear of winning. Pushing off for the last lap of the 200 individual medley, she shot a glance at the other lanes and saw not a single soul: She was completely in the lead. She could win the race. But while she'd envisioned swimming a great race, she hadn't at all planned on winning. Winning would mean going directly to Seoul for the Games, and—the thought raced through her mind—she hadn't even gotten herself a passport. *I haven't packed!* she told herself. *I don't have enough underwear! And what about school!*

That momentary fear was just enough to cost her the race. First or second place would have taken her to the Olympics; she came in third. She missed placing by twenty-seven one-hundredths of a second.

Fear of success takes on many forms. I've known managers who've gotten themselves passed over for promotion out of fear that a leadership position might alienate them from their former peers or even force them into the position of having to fire some of them. I've known realtors who passed on lucrative new accounts because they feared they'd have to overhaul themselves—new clothing, new car, new work habits—in order to "fit in" with an upscale clientele. I worked with an author who had a wicked case of writer's block because she was afraid another successful novel would raise expectations of her even higher. And a deputy district attorney I counseled actually feared winning a high-profile case because she wasn't ready to handle the media intrusion.

You get the idea: Success has a ripplelike effect. Not knowing what will be affected, or fearing that the consequences will be negative, is why people sometimes fear doing their best.

The consequence most feared, interestingly, is a negative impact on one's social life. Leaving friends behind, having less time with family, having fame destroy the easy rapport with colleagues and strangers—these are the worries that get in the way of winning. Some competitors I've counseled don't want to have to edge out the competition.

This was certainly the case with Steve Shelton, the Grand Prix driver whom I mentioned in the previous chapter. Steve was an awfully nice guy. He was in the habit, before a race, of going from trailer to trailer to schmooze and shoot the bull with the other drivers—guys he was about to go head-to-head with in a very dangerous arena. He liked being liked. He wanted to beat out these other guys, but he didn't want to have it cost him his friendships, or his reputation of being a nice guy.

I told him if he developed a killer instinct, he would win. But I also let him know that this didn't entail a personality change. I asked him about his pre-race routine. He said he didn't have one, other than this going from trailer to trailer to hang out with the other drivers. So we started with that: no more visiting. For the half hour or so before the race, he was to isolate himself in his trailer, get centered, and mentally rehearse the first ten laps. Then he was to dress himself in a ritualistic way—the same order each time. First the Nomex fireproof underwear. Then his uniform. Then his shoes. Then his gloves.

The ritual would allow him the single-mindedness he needed to focus on winning. But it served another purpose, one we've just discussed with regard to Anthony and his fear of failing as a salesman: Putting on his uniform was like putting on a costume. Steve was assuming a new role, much as an actor would put himself into a mindset to get into his character.

By the time he put on his helmet, he had made a complete transformation. No more Mr. Nice Guy. He was now a fierce competitor. No one looking at him could see Steve Shelton anymore. The very feel of the fireproof underwear, the very sound of the uniform's zipper, became process cues, signals to shift over into the mind-set with the killer instinct.

"I was out there to win," Steve commented. "As long as I was wearing that uniform, I was out there to put people away."

If you suspect that what's holding you back is something similar—a nice-guy complex, as I call it—try another exercise. Try putting on paper all your worries and concerns about winning what you want. Try to anticipate every possible ripple that success might make in your personal and professional life. Once again, seeing your concerns in black and white is the first step in defusing their power over you: Now they're in your control, in a manageable list. Spend some time thinking how you might handle each item on the list, each ripple effect. Chances are you'll convince yourself you *will* handle them. Half the battle is just putting a name to these formless anxieties. When you know them and can plan for them, they can't jump out and scare you at the worst possible moment.

Trust in Yourself . . . and Go for It

There comes a point when all this training is ready to be put to the test. You'll feel strong. You'll feel ready to trust in your talent, your training, your experience, and the voice that says, "I can." There will come a test, a challenge, a performance of some kind—and you will choose to undertake it.

Once you've made that choice, then commit to it and go for it. As the Nike ad goes, *just do it.*

I can remember my first parachute jump with the Green Berets. I hadn't made a jump since Ranger School, more than six months earlier. Sitting at the open door with my feet on the skids, I looked at the distance to the ground. I thought how little margin for error I had, and for a split second, I wondered if I would choose, as one of my buddies did, to stay rooted to the cabin floor. But above the deafening *thwap* of the rotors I heard the jumpmaster yell, "Go!" I said, "Geronimo!," which for some reason we were trained to say, and I took the leap into thin air.

I trusted my training and equipment. I let go. It was hugely exhilarating. Courage is, as they say, its own reward.

This chapter has taken you through a training program designed to bring you to this same moment of trust and letting go. It comprises a series of exercises to build, progressively, your courage, your self-confidence, and above all, your awareness that whatever success you envision is yours if you only dare to risk going after it. I've laid out a path of steps that should take you to the edge of your comfort zone, without ever scaring you to the point of forcing your retreat. Starting with baby steps, you learn to walk before you try running.

But once you've completed that path, and once you've resolved to run, I say *go for it*. No hesitating. No second-guessing yourself. No further analysis. No holding back at the last instant. Trust in yourself and your training. And here's why: In virtually every arena, tentativeness blows the performance. You can suffer injury, defeat, even death if at the last minute you decide to play it safe, or hold back, or take a baby step where a committed stride was called for.

Golfers are fond of saying, "Ninety-nine percent of short putts don't go in." Putts become short when golfers become tentative, when they allow fear to constrict their muscles so they make a small, choppy movement. The ball falls short of the hole. But with a bold stroke, even a ball hit too hard still has a chance of dropping in.

I say practice the bold stroke over and over in normal play and then, when you're feeling the heat of competition, *commit to making that stroke right before you step up to the ball*.

For springboard divers, the consequences of getting tentative at the last possible second are somewhat graver. Fear tends to make them baby the last step of their hurdle, the step that gives them the bounce and elevation they need to execute the dive and clear the board. Pushing off that last step too hard could only send them farther out into the pool, but fear misleads them. They hold back. They don't reach the end of the board. And they risk hitting the board and incurring serious injury.

For race car drivers, failure to commit to the bold course of action can be absolutely fatal. There's something called "trailing throttle oversteer," which is the tendency of untrained drivers to go into a curve fast and, out of panic, ease up on the throttle. You've probably experienced just such a reflex. Speeding down a highway, you see your exit too late and take the cloverleaf too fast. What did you do? Midturn, you braked. If you were lucky, you stayed on the road. But thousands of off-ramp guardrails can attest to the fact that braking on a curve is the wrong thing to do. Braking sends the car's weight to the front, making the rear "light." You're in the middle of a turn, but the light rear end is still traveling forward at high speed. Braking can put you into a tailspin.

Race car drivers don't even need to touch the brakes to throw themselves into a tailspin. Just trailing off the throttle is enough to land them in the middle of a curve broadside to the other drivers. In fact, the safest way to get through a curve is to do just the opposite of what instinct demands, and that is to hit the accelerator. So race car drivers train to overcome instinct. Over and over they practice going into turns, going faster and faster with each repetition, and at precisely the moment self-preservation insists they back off the pedal, they step on it.

In other words, the gutsiest action is by far the safest, and fastest, way to navigate a kink in the road.

No matter what your career road, doubtless you've encountered quite a few of these twists already. I can bet if you panicked and hit the brakes, you spun out. But I've shown you how to ignore the counsel of fear. With practice and training, you can navigate the next turns with the kind of boldness that will send you through like a slingshot.

SUMMARY

Courage is feeling afraid and taking action anyway. This ability to risk is something we all have. Every day we take actions where we might have opted to do nothing. But either we don't count these actions as courageous or we don't remember the risks we have taken and the fear we have overcome. Hence when under pressure to perform, our fears—fear of failure, of humiliation, of success—keep us from performing our best. As a result of giving in to fear, our confidence suffers. And success eludes us.

The training set forth in this chapter is designed to build trust in yourself—enough to impel you to act, even in the face of fear. The exercises are like a set of workout weights; they graduate in heaviness. In ascending order they are:

* The **Courage Journal**—creating a record of past initiatives, risks taken, and other acts of courage
* The **Courage Log**—keeping a day-to-day listing of current bold moves or initiatives
* **Using symbols**—finding talismans of past success and displaying them or keeping them handy as instant reminders
* **Learning to be assertive**—following the three-step guidelines to staging and scripting difficult conversations and getting the results you want
* **Using your humor**—putting yourself at ease by thinking of something funny, or by putting others at ease by making them laugh
* **Acting as if**—assuming the dress, manner, speech, attitude, and bearing of the gutsy person you'd like to be
* **Committing to go for it**—trusting in yourself enough to resist tentative action and give it your all instead

For your personalized Courage Plan, turn to Appendix D.

CHAPTER FIVE

Focus: How to Get Past Distraction

Nothing interferes with my concentration.
You could put on an orgy in my office and I
wouldn't look up. Well, maybe once.

—ISAAC ASIMOV

As long as he was negotiating multimillion-dollar real estate deals, Cal*, thirty-four, a corporate finance VP at a major San Francisco insurance firm, was calm, cool, and very collected.

But when it came time to go before the executive committee and convince them to underwrite one of his transactions, Cal felt inwardly out of control. His heart raced. His voice quavered. He perspired right through his deodorant. Random, irrelevant thoughts buzzed in his head like bees in a jar. He could not focus on the task at hand—only on the consequences of failing to perform in line with his superiors' expectations.

Cal was baffled as to how he could have come this far in terms of responsibility and title and still be subject to such fears and distress. He was tough; he'd been on the fast track ever since graduating from a Division One college where he started as a defensive end.

"I've achieved a lot," he told me when we first met. "People trust me. I actually have a reputation as a good public speaker. So why on earth do I feel these levels of anxiety?"

Fearing that if he didn't get a grip on his inner turmoil, he'd blow his reputation for coolheadedness, Cal consulted a lot of books on overcoming presentation jitters. He enrolled in Toastmasters to get the practice the books insisted would help him.

But practice didn't help, because he was addressing the wrong issue. His anxiety and nervous energy weren't the enemy to overcome. They simply needed to be channeled. Harnessed.

Focused.

Cal got this insight after he took the Seven Skills Survey. (If you've not completed it, go back to the Introduction; the scores in this factor are very important.)

"It was clear I was having trouble staying in the moment," he noted. "My mind would rush ahead of what I was doing and play through a disaster scenario, which caused me even more concern, making my thoughts spin even faster. I couldn't concentrate."

What Is Focus?

If I were to say that being able to concentrate is one of life's most critical skills, no one would argue, I'm sure. We esteem it all the more these days because it's in such short supply. Our frantic, frenetic, multitasking lifestyles conspire against giving our full attention to any one thing, so it seems we are losing the capacity to *focus*. It appears our children are in danger of never developing that capacity; to hear psychiatrists tell it, attention deficit disorder is epidemic. Prescriptions for Prozac and Ritalin are on the rise, even among the very young. Bookstore shelves are groaning with books on ADD—its symptoms, its pharmaceutical therapies, and the factors that put certain individuals at risk.

But notice we're fixated on the disorder, not the cure.

Whenever I lecture on the topic, I always put this question to my audience: "Can anyone name the four aspects of focus?" No one ever has a clue. No one volunteers even a guess. No one understands how to improve one's focus, only how to diagnose its absence. And so it remains a major stumbling block even for guys like Cal, who've made it to the top of the corporate food chain.

Fact is, even if Cal had perceived focus to be his problem and looked for books to help him learn how to rein in his thoughts under pressure, he wouldn't have found any he could readily understand. They're not written for anyone but academics, and they're not very practical.

I grew up an athlete, a diver for whom concentration might mean the difference between a clean dive and a spinal cord injury. Yet it was assumed, throughout my training, that I was born with this skill, or I'd somehow acquire it by my own trial-and-error process. When I was in my early twenties, a guy I met on a beach volleyball court got me reading the Eastern philosophers and martial-arts masters. I wrestled with the unfamiliar language. What concepts I could grasp, I had difficulty putting into practice. Even when my doctoral dissertation hooked me up with Robert Nideffer, the world's leading authority on attentional theory, I found that the same gap persisted between academic understanding and clinical practice.

I was determined to close that gap. I wrote a book of my own, but more important, I field-tested my ideas on my clients. I taught them:

* *Presence*—how to stay in the moment, and not leap ahead or drift into the past
* *Intensity*—how to train 100 percent of their energies on the object or task at hand
* *Duration*—how to sustain their focus past external distraction for as long as the task required it

* *Mental quiet*—how to remain undistracted by internal noise or imagery

Together, these skills comprise *focus*—the ability to concentrate fully on one person, object, task, feeling, or concept for as long as necessary.

By the end of this chapter, you, too, will have learned to concentrate. I'm going to give you **a whole tool chest of strategies to get you into the present moment; to get your focus to the level at which you perform best; to sustain that focus past all distraction; and to get past mental noise,** past thinking, to that magical place where you are of such single-minded purpose and action that there is no distinction between yourself and the object of your focus.

If this sounds like work, it is.

But I promise you, the payoff will more than compensate you for your effort.

Presence

When I met Cammie*, twenty-eight, she had just failed her state medical board for the second time.

"I had no trouble concentrating on the test," she explained to me. "It's the *studying* that's a problem. All that memorizing is so humdrum, so repetitious, I get bored. I daydream. Just a word I come across in the text can send me off."

To learn how to focus, Cammie had to first learn how to stay in the moment, on the task at hand. Her thoughts were like unruly children who'd been told to sit still in the center of a room. They kept wandering off, forgetting what had been asked of them. Staying in the moment is in fact a discipline. But there are ways to make it easier.

ELIMINATING EXTERNAL DISTRACTIONS

The first step for Cammie was to eliminate the Pied Pipers whom her children kept following. She needed to determine what was luring away her thoughts as she studied. I gave her a very simple exercise to begin with. In the space of a half hour she was to write down everything that distracted her while she was trying to memorize material for the exam. Every time she switched study environments, she was to get out a new piece of paper.

At first she wouldn't do it. "I know what I thought about," she insisted. "I know how often I got off course. I don't need a piece of paper to remind me."

But when she started writing down the distractions she encountered in each different place she studied, she was surprised at what she learned.

"It made me so much more aware of my environment," she said. "If I was on my terrace, with the dog loose, the birds out, I'd see the result: I didn't remember much of what I'd studied. I did much better on the subway, believe it or not. Or in my living room—with the animals locked up—where I couldn't go off on a daydream every time some guy walked down the street."

The better you can know what's causing your thoughts to wander off, the better you'll be able to come up with appropriate strategies to thwart them—such as avoiding certain environments altogether. Make a written inventory of every attention-breaker. You may find, as Cammie did, that just the exercise of writing imposes a discipline on your thoughts.

"The blank piece of paper became a competitive thing for me," she notes. "It became a challenge with myself, not to have to write anything down. I'd focus better just so I could end the half hour with an unmarked sheet of paper."

CREATING ATTENTIONAL BOUNDARIES

Another strategy is to put up an imaginary barrier around you—what I call an *attentional boundary*. Through this barrier, no distracting sound or movement can affect you; and likewise, your attention is contained within the space it encompasses. The more visual you make it, the more effective it will be. Remember the "cone of silence," that plastic shield in the television spoof *Get Smart?* The Chief lowered it on himself and Agent Maxwell Smart whenever he wanted total privacy; you can lower one of your own whenever you want to seal out unwanted distraction. It can be a protective wall, bubble, dome, or cone; one of my opera singers used to "zip herself into" a plastic egg before going on stage, to keep out all the coughing and candy-wrapper noise that tended to interfere with her concentration. Another of my clients, a thirty-seven-year-old voice-over artist we'll call Bill*, borrowed from his travels in England the image of a medieval castle room, richly carpeted and tapestried, whose fortresslike walls permitted no noise or conversation to distract him. We'll be talking more about Bill in just a moment.

CENTERING FOR PRESENCE

Finally, there's the process of centering to give you practice in staying in the here and now. Imagine a circle with a dot in the center. You occupy this circle while centering; everything outside of centering remains outside the circle. The dot is your breathing. Your breathing is your focus, the task at hand, the thing that fills the present moment. It's not much of a task, in that normally it's something you do without thinking—but now you are to be aware of it and nothing else. At first this will be difficult. Your thoughts will wander out of the circle, and you'll follow them. But you're not a child; you're the parent. Gently steer your thoughts back into the circle, to the very center, where you need them to focus on breathing. Over and over you'll have to herd them into the circle, but as you work at it, they'll obey. You'll start to get compliance. With practice you'll learn to become totally present, utterly in the here and now, all of you. It's a powerful feeling. And indeed, when you are there, you are at your most powerful.

Intensity

Breathing is not a task that requires much power. In fact, I can't think of any action that requires *less* energy than breathing. As tasks go, it's an effortless one.

But most every other task requires energy. To give 100 percent of your attention to accomplishing the task at hand is very taxing. Some critical projects require such intensity that we are thoroughly drained afterward. The more intense your focus, and the longer you engage it, the more reserves of energy you'll empty.

So the first aspect of intensity is energy. Giving your whole self to performing a task requires a lot of it. You cannot expect to perform well if you cannot summon the energy.

Often, as in Cal's case, the problem going into a performance isn't a lack of energy; it's a lack of control. Hence the second aspect of intensity is control. Total focus requires both the intensity and the narrowness of a laser beam. If you can harness the voltage, using it to narrow your focus into a precision tool instead of feeling it scatter your thoughts, you'll be absolutely electric. Riveting. You will command the attention of your audience in the act of focusing your own.

A presentation, it should be noted, is a performance you prepare for. You plan out the way in which you'll get yourself rested and ready to give 100 percent. Sure it demands energy, but it's not a chronic drain. Most performances in the business world, however, are chronic: Each workday is a series of miniperformances—critical phone calls, deal negotiations, client meetings. Often there's no time to prepare, because there's no knowing when you'll next need to be "on." There isn't much downtime built into the day to recharge for the repeated assaults on your attention. Additionally, there isn't much room for error. A lapse in focus, a failure of intensity, could translate into a patient dying, a window of opportunity closing, millions of dollars lost.

The higher you are in the food chain, the more chronic your performance demands—and the more energy you'll need to expend on focusing.

No one can sustain his concentration at full intensity for a ten-hour day, day after day. Superman himself would be out cold if he applied his X-ray vision for longer than a few minutes at a stretch. If you try to sustain intense focus throughout your day, you will invariably run out of energy and won't be able to focus when you need to most.

Better to pace yourself. If you were running a marathon, you wouldn't dare try to sprint for twenty-six miles. You'll have the energy to concentrate on demand throughout the day if you take an interval-training approach to conserving and expending the energy that total focus demands. If you've ever put in time on a StairMaster, you know what I mean; you want to choose the program that looks like this:

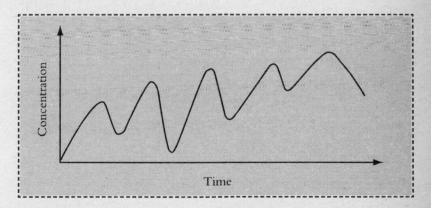

rather than the one that maps a workout like the one on page 128.

You can't peak if you don't drop; it's just one of those laws of nature. To be able to concentrate intensely, you must take advantage of any letup in the action to recharge your battery.

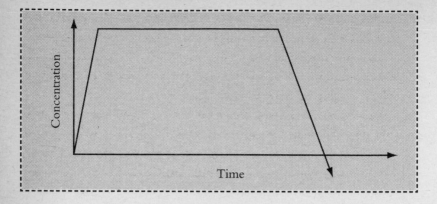

Allocate Your Energy Wisely

It helps to recognize, and exploit, your own particular cycles of energy. If you were to map out your energy highs and lows over a sixteen-hour period, I'll bet it looks a lot like that StairMaster interval program, with peaks, plateaus, and valleys. Try to allocate the most demanding work of your day—the work that demands the most concentration—to those periods when you naturally find yourself more energetic. If a lot of your high plateaus and peaks fall in the morning, make sure you don't fritter away that period on pick-and-shovel tasks like paying bills, answering e-mail, or chatting on the phone. Work that doesn't require much focus can be done when you don't have the mental energy to give to it.

HOW TO RALLY ENERGY FOR FOCUS: CENTERING UP

There are going to be times when you're languishing in an energy trough and get called upon to perform. A crisis knocks on your door at 4:00 P.M., oblivious to the fact you've spent the morning putting out fires, and you need to find the energy to rally your full attention to resolve it. Or you wish there *were* a crisis, because pressure helps to focus you, and in the absence of pressure you can't rally. Your mind wanders, and it's costing you.

Either way, centering can help you crank up your energy level to help you focus intensely. In Chapter Two we discussed how to center *down;* now we're going to review how to center *up.*

1. Start out with a clear intention and a focal point. But instead of sitting down, **stand with your knees well flexed,** to get blood surging in your quadriceps.

2. Instead of taking measured breaths in through the nose and out through the mouth, **breathe forcefully, in and out, through your mouth.** Don't hyperventilate; three to five breaths should do it.

3. While you're breathing hard, with your arms at your side, **pump your hands into fists and let go** several times.

4. Drop all the tension you just induced in your forearms and shoulders. Shake them out.

5. Find your center.

6. Feel the energy pooled there, or imagine it forming a pool, and **repeat your process cue.**

7. Shoot that energy up from your center and out your eyes to your focal point.

Now go *kick ass.*

If this reminds you of how sprinters and swimmers behave before a race, it should. At the sound of the gun, they've got to be at full rev, not half-speed. They need to leave the blocks in high gear. So do you.

Centering up induces the kind of pumping heart and flood of energy that adrenaline gives you, even when adrenaline fails to kick in. And yes, when you're dog-tired, or when you've been dosed with adrenaline surges for the past six hours, adrenaline can fail to give you the kick you need. We've all experienced times when what we need is a fire lit under us, and we can't even get a spark. That's when centering up can help.

There are other ways. Try to spark yourself with a challenge. Invent a pressure situation for yourself. Or go take a really brisk walk, or run up and down the stairs. Dash your face with cold water. Drink coffee. Whatever reliably gets you going, do it. Because intensity takes energy.

HOW TO NARROW THE BEAM: VISUALIZATION

By now you should know how to modulate your energy to meet the demands of a performance situation. If you can't focus intensely because you're low on energy, then you know how to rev up by centering up. If, on the other hand, your energy is so high that focus is next to impossible, you need to center down to get that voltage under control.

Once you've got the voltage optimal, it's a matter of training it into a beam. The technique is called *visualization*. Visualize either what it is you want to do (for instance, speak authoritatively and persuasively) or some place or person or thing that will put you in the frame of mind that will help you perform as you wish.

Cal found it extremely helpful to train his mind's eye on the individual faces he was about to confront in the conference room. "I'd see them right in front of me, so close I could see all their wrinkles and smell their breath," he explains. "That gave me a sense of their humanity. It's being away from people that's intimidating. As soon as I could see them as they are, I could see myself smiling, speaking passionately, enjoying myself—and being totally in that moment."

At other times, Cal envisioned himself sitting by a cool, clear pool of water. He imagined himself perched on a sunny rock, looking into the pool, studying the rocks on the bottom, feeling the sun on his neck and the coolness of the water on his fingertips. "I've gotten so I can relax just by visualizing that peaceful place," he says.

Bill, the voice-over guy I introduced earlier in this chapter, told me this whole exercise was just too "touchy-feely" for him. He was having trouble feeling his center; he didn't see the point of working at the imagery. But after a period of resistance, during which he found his relaxation skills improving, he turned his career around by using visualization.

Bill made his living reading books on tape, doing voice-overs for commercials, narrating documentaries and the like. He had a great voice and excellent diction, but he wasn't getting the work he wanted because his readings sounded too much alike. He sounded too wooden.

We want more energy, he'd hear. *We need a sparkling, effervescent delivery. The tone needs to be brighter. The pace needs to be faster.*

"So I'd tell myself, *Be energized,*" Bill reflects, "but if anything, that made me more apprehensive. You can't impose enthusiasm on a script; it has to grow out of you, out of your experience."

Exactly right. You can't *tell* yourself how to sound. We've already explored how ineffective the left brain is when it comes to inspiring you to act. It has just the opposite effect. But if you can engage the right brain, which relies on pictures rather than words, you can *show* yourself what it is you want to do. By now it should be pretty obvious that, to your mind, a picture's worth volumes of instruction.

Bill came up with several visuals that conveyed the quality he wanted his voice to have. One was a July 4 sparkler; in his mind he'd focus on the white burning end of it, the point that kept sprouting sparks. Throughout the reading, he'd have this image before his mind's eye. Another was the image and sound of a train racing by him on a platform; by focusing on the silver flash of cars going by, he "experienced" the sensation of speed. Because it was in his mind, he found he could even regulate how fast the cars were going. The third visual he relied on, especially when auditioning for instructional videos, was an image of a white-coated instructor standing at a blackboard in front of a room of students. "I'd focus on the students until I could feel their attention on the instructor," Bill explained, "and then I knew I was ready to be that instructor."

He incorporated the visuals into his centering routine. Before he set foot in the sound studio, he closed his eyes, released the tension he always found in his laryngeal muscles, relaxed his neck and shoulders, and tried to find his center. It was difficult for him to find it, but with practice he got better at it. "Just assuming it was there helped me relax," he says. "I'd get to that spot, that ground zero, and then I'd load the image I needed."

To keep his focus trained on that image, and to help him keep irrelevant thoughts and images at bay, Bill imposed his attentional boundary—the dark, fortresslike castle room. When it came time to "load" his image, Bill imagined a screen lowering before him as he sat in this protected place. When it came time to record, Bill was ready. He was up, he was energized, and that energy was so focused he was absolutely riveting. Powerful. Intense.

"I had thought I needed to be perfect or they wouldn't call me back," Bill reflects. "But being perfect doesn't make for a good performance; taking risks, indulging in my character, being spontaneous does. I am absolutely *loving* my work now."

Duration

You've learned by now how to get in the present moment. You've learned how to find, tap, and direct energy to the task of focusing intensely. Now it's time to sustain that intensity. Now it's time to learn how to prolong the duration of your focus.

VISUAL DURATION

Try this one-minute exercise. Choose a focal point, like the flame of a candle or the period at the end of this sentence, and see if you can keep your gaze on just the point of the flame or the dot for sixty seconds. Don't let your eye take in the wick or the candle, or the sentence or the page—or what lies beyond them or below them. Try not to let your thoughts wander beyond what information your eyes are taking in; let everything else drop away. Stay in the moment. Gaze intently.

This isn't easy. I'll bet you're drifting in less than thirty seconds. It's said that children have an attention span of up to four seconds; most adults can stay focused for only about six; and Zen masters, upwards of twelve. But keep at it. With practice you can become a Zen master.

AUDITORY DURATION

Try focusing on a single sound pulled out of the background you're immersed in right now—perhaps the hum of your computer, a distant phone ringing, or the tick of your watch. Bend your full attention to hearing it. The minute you do, of course, you'll be keenly aware of just how many *other* little sounds contribute to your environment. But see if you can stay with that one chosen sound a full minute, to the exclusion of seeing, feeling, tasting, hearing, or thinking about anything else.

KINESTHETIC DURATION

Practice focusing your attention on a feeling, a sensation, or a movement. Breathing is a good choice. Feeling your center is another. Releasing muscle tension is yet another. See if you can direct and sustain your focus on any one of these internal feelings. Ignore all the belly gurgles or chest heaves that vie for your sensory attention. Stay focused on the sensation for as long as you can.

ADVERSITY TRAINING

Once you feel you've got the hang of sustaining your focus on a sight, a sound, or a feeling, it's time to combine the visual, auditory, and sensory distractions vying for your attention. Try preparing your taxes with your kids running around the room, or with the television going or someone talking on the phone. Try rehearsing a speech with the radio tuned to a talk station or music you can't stand. Try finding your center when you're jogging up a steep hill and your legs and lungs are about to give out. Layer on distractions—sights, sounds, sensations—one by one, until you can sustain your focus despite all of them going at once.

It's a form of adversity training, because adversity is the environment in which you'll be called upon to perform.

When I was in Colorado working with junior golfers, I put together a putting contest for the kids. They played eighteen holes. I got some fancy prizes donated by local merchants to inspire the competition. Then I told the members of each foursome to go all out in terms of distracting whoever was hitting a shot. I encouraged them to jump up and down, practice their swings, crack jokes, make noises, make conversation—whatever they could think of to get the player's mind off his stroke. They did a super job; the first few holes were disasters. But by the eleventh hole a lot of the kids had figured out how to perform despite those distractions. And by the sixteenth hole none of the foursomes were even bothering to talk and jump around anymore, because it wasn't working.

Adversity training hones not just your ability to sustain an intense focus; it also builds your confidence. The more distraction you manage to overcome in practice sessions, the more confident you'll feel about your ability to focus anytime, anywhere, under any circumstances. No matter how intense the stress of performance or the tedium of preparation, you'll know you have triumphed over worse.

Mental Quiet

If you're distracted only by what you see or hear or feel going on *around* you, consider yourself lucky. When the distraction you see or hear or feel is *right inside your head,* it's harder to get past it.

Take negative self-talk—the Scrooge voice, as Cammie, the med student, came to call her inner critic. As we discussed in the chapter on perspective, self-talk has the power to sabotage your performance precisely because it's so distracting. You can't concentrate on the task at hand when your left brain is muttering things like, *You can't do this. You're not up to this. You don't stand a chance. You're not smart enough. You're way out of your league here.* The left brain has unerring radar for just the words and phrases that will poke through your defenses and rattle you.

Cammie's left-brain chatter undermined her motivation to stick with her course of study. ("It's hard to concentrate when you think what you're doing is futile," she commented.)

As if unceasing critical commentary weren't distracting enough, the right brain can take any lapse in focus as an opportunity to project frightful video clips on your mental screen. These aren't necessarily taken from your past; they're often conjured on the spot with vivid material from your imagination. In the blink of an eye the right brain can show you your entire life unraveling, your worst fears materializing. The right brain provides you with a perverse focus if you don't impose one of your own choosing.

Steve Shelton, the race car driver I worked with, was particularly prone to right-brain sabotage as he sat waiting for the "go" light at the start of a race. (In certain Formula races, drivers assume different starting positions on a track grid and start from a full stop.) Instead of focusing on the green light and the split-second series of moves he'd need to execute to get off to a good start, Steve allowed horrible movies to play across his consciousness. He'd seen friends get killed at the start because they'd stalled out or failed to get under way before drivers behind them plowed into them. It didn't take much to imagine himself a sitting duck. The more he saw these scenarios, the more distracted he became, and the more self-fulfilling his fears of starting poorly turned out to be. He burned out clutches and tires. He jumped the light. He lost precious seconds even though his qualifying time had often put him ahead of the other drivers in the grid.

"My whole problem was lack of focus," he noted. "I couldn't control my thoughts while I was in the car, and in racing, you've got to be single-minded. There isn't room, or time, for any extraneous thoughts."

Learning to focus past *internal* distraction—whether it's right-brain doomsday videos or left-brain chatter—requires a multifaceted approach.

One approach we already explored in the perspective chapter. You need to tell the distracting voices to shut up. You first must become conscious of them, as Cammie did with her writing exercise. Once you know what they are, you can distance yourself from them—the "I" vs. "you" perspective. You can develop a relationship with them, one in which the I takes an authoritative stance with the you. Cammie named her distracting voices Scrooge, the one that kept telling her she wasn't smart enough, and Mr. Bojangles, the voice that tempted her to put down her books and go follow him to the park or the pizza joint or out with her friends instead of studying. Naming them helped her say, *I'm busy now, I'll talk to you later*—or, with Scrooge, *It's not your life anymore, it's mine.* She found it very helpful.

Similarly, you can have your right brain substitute old highlight films for those awful doomsday videos. Or you can create new highlight films using mental rehearsal, as Steve Shelton did. These two strategies I also explained in Chapter Three.

The strategy I want to explore in detail here hinges on getting out of the instructional mode, and getting away from left-brain words altogether, in order to achieve what I call mental quiet. Total focus requires total mental quiet, and a brain that's analyzing and commenting isn't quiet. A brain that engages in verbal thought processes—even if it's to instruct itself to focus—is distracted.

But how to get beyond thought?

By engaging in a set of *ritualized* actions.

THE PRE-EVENT ROUTINE

Think for a minute about the circumstances under which you come up with your best ideas, or solutions to problems that have been plaguing you. Is it while you're driving on an open highway? On back roads? While you're taking a long hot shower? Are you able to get the big picture by staring into the surf? Into a fire? Do you feel like you can get a handle on a difficult situation after a long run or an hour shoveling snow? Does music on the commute to work put your mind in order? Or do you get your best game plan for the next day while chopping vegetables for dinner?

Ritual, or repetitive action, has a lulling effect on the left brain. Like the swinging watch used by hypnotists, it lulls the conscious mind into a quiet state. Quite literally, brain waves shift from high-frequency, high-amplitude, beta waves to flatter, longer alpha waves. Alpha waves account for that mellow, peaceful sensation you have right before drifting asleep or just before you open your eyes in the morning—what's called reverie—before the left brain starts firing and a thousand thoughts crowd your consciousness. By engaging in a ritual that's strongly visual, kinesthetic, or auditory, you are disengaging your left brain, because it simply doesn't have the skills to process this kind of input. You're shifting to right-brain mode, the nonverbal, nonanalytical, intuitive and creative mind.

A good pre-event routine consists of actions that immerse you in the sort of sensory input only your right brain can process. Once you've made the switch, once you've silenced the mental noise, single-mindedness—the holy grail of concentration—is within your grasp.

I'll give you a very commonplace example of a simple but effective pre-event routine. Watch a tennis pro serve. Watch what he does before he hits the ball. Maybe he bounces the ball a couple times on the baseline. Maybe he rocks back and forth in a measured rhythm. He most certainly eyes his intended target, that corner of the service box that his opponent can't reach. His whole pre-serve routine may take only a few seconds, but I guarantee he has one. And I guarantee he's not using it to perform computations or analyze the particulars of his swing. No, the bouncing, the rocking of his feet together, serve to reconnect him to the *sensations* involved in hitting a great serve. He's leaving his left brain. He's getting into the ball so that at the moment he releases it, he and the ball and his intended target are *one*.

Left-brain thoughts play no part in this complex synchronization of actions. If they did—if the player were to suddenly wonder if he'd put together a high enough toss, a loose enough grip, an angled enough racket—he'd probably whiff the ball, much less get the serve in.

A Model Pre-Event Routine

In the previous chapter I introduced you to Anthony, the advertising exec who made a commercial go of his fine-arts avocation by acting as if he were Picasso whenever he made a sales call. Even before he lacked the courage to sell his work, however, he lacked the focus to produce it. When I met him, he was enormously frustrated because he had this three-day weekend in which to paint but he simply couldn't get "in the groove." The minute he confronted the blank canvas, a steady stream of doubts and fears rushed in to distract him.

What is the matter with you? You've waited all week for this, and now you can't think what to paint?
You're wasting time. Precious time!
What is that? Is that the best you can do?
Do you see the time?
That really sucks.
What makes you think you, at your age, are going to suddenly make it?
Face it. This is never going to get you anywhere.

Anthony wasted practically every Saturday just trying to get past this noise. That fueled his panic that, come Monday, he'd have nothing to show for his weekend before heading into the workweek. That in turn fueled his fear that he was never going to break out of the day job he'd come to hate.

I asked Anthony what he did to warm up. Did he sketch? Listen to music? Visualize what he wanted to paint?

"I make phone calls, make myself another cup of coffee, even do laundry," he admitted. "I fritter. I guess I thought that *was* my way of warming up."

The first stage of the pre-event routine I devised for Anthony began before he even opened the door to his studio. He listened to classical music—baroque in particular. He spent a few minutes centering—breathing, relaxing, and visualizing. With his eyes closed, he envisioned the painting session as he would like it to go. He walked himself through an ideal morning, in his head. He visualized himself painting fluidly, flowingly, getting the images down with ease. And of course, he visualized what he wanted to paint in vivid colors.

Once he'd mentally rehearsed the morning as he wanted it to go, he could go into his studio. Yet instead of going right to his easel, I had him spend some time with his paints and palette. I told him to play with his paints—squeeze them out, stick his fingers in them, *feel* them in addition to seeing their colors.

Still, he wasn't to put brush to canvas. I had him take yesterday's palette, or a board or piece of paper, and use that to warm up. I emphasized it was to be a "throwaway," a purely-for-practice piece. It didn't count. It was just for fun, just for warm-up.

We imposed no time limit on his warm-up period; I told him not to wear a watch. Instead, he set a kitchen timer to ring after forty-five minutes, to remind him it was time for a break.

Meanwhile, as he dabbled in his paints, I had him play George Carlin tapes. And on the studio walls, wherever his glance might happen to fall, I had him post giant signs painted with one word: YES.

If a lot of this sounds silly, it's because it was intended to be. Anthony desperately needed to lighten up. He was totally in the thrall of his left brain, which, after all, called the shots from Tuesday through Friday. For twenty-two years the left-brain drill sergeant had been in charge. It got him to be productive, efficient, and deadline-driven. He'd used its critical faculties to make his work and that of his department responsive to client needs. He was a successful exec in large part because of his left brain's dominance.

But when it came to painting for himself—not for any client, not on any deadline, not for any dollar figure—the flogging voice of the left brain was not only inappropriate, it was beating the spark out of his passion. It kept trying to get Anthony to perform the way an overbearing parent hopes to get a child to behave: through fear of the consequences.

Fear can motivate. But it certainly doesn't inspire. Which is why Anthony's pre-event routine had to be silly. He needed to be made to laugh. Lighten up. Goof around. Play. Together, the visual stimulus (the YES signs), the auditory (the George Carlin comedy tapes), and the sensual (dabbling in the wet paint) conspired to usher the overbearing, threatening parent from the studio.

"I'd look up and see those YES signs," Anthony said, "and I could feel this big, stupid grin spreading across my face. I didn't have to push away any negative thoughts or critical comments—how could I have any?"

And a funny thing happened.

Anthony's warm-up pieces weren't winding up in the trash bin.

"The first couple I wiped clean or threw out," he told me. "But then I put them on the wall and looked at them. And they were new, new, new!

"I got into a flow I'd never experienced before," he continued. "My work was changing, and it was shocking! Exciting! I couldn't wait to get into my studio each morning. The stuff in my head just poured out."

Putting Together Your Own Pre-Event Routine

Now take a good, hard look at the way in which you prepare to do your best work—whether it's negotiating a contract, writing a script or acting it out, presenting information, or making a decision.

How do you prepare? Do you tend to do the same things each time? Do you do the *right* things each time?

My golfing friend John Golden thought he did. "I've seen the pros," he told me when we first met. "My pre-shot routine is like theirs." Then he described how he calculated what club to use, and how he'd stand over the ball thinking about his grip, his stance, and where he wanted his right elbow during his swing.

I got John to pick his club and then, about ten feet from the ball, stand behind it and center until he felt his shoulders relax. Instead of eyeing the target and making computations, he was to simply visualize the flight or path of the ball toward it. I had him take practice swings until he "felt" the one he wanted to use. As soon as he did, he was to step up to the ball and hit it—focusing only on the target, not his swing.

That year he won both the Colorado State Match Play championship and the Medal Play championship. "It was the missing ingredient, that pre-shot routine," John mused. "I hadn't realized that it was a *mental* preparation, not a mechanical one."

The routines athletes use to get them into an alpha-wave state of mental quiet are, not surprisingly, very kinesthetic. Their routine focuses them on a feeling—the feel of a good toss, the feel of a good jump, the feel of a smooth swing.

It makes sense, too, that my Juilliard students devise pre-event routines that rely on auditory cues—the sound of their opening phrase as they'd like to play it, or the sound of the most challenging part played well.

But the best routines, like that which I devised for Anthony, are multisensory. They employ sounds, visuals, and sensations to "cue" the right brain to assume command and silence the left-brain noise that interferes with single-minded action.

Study your own work environment. Before you step into it, or before you make a phone call, turn to a screen, or report to a room full of people, consider what rituals might help you make the mental shift you need to be single-minded for your intended action. You may find it helpful to incorporate some or all of the following components:

Centering: The seven steps may be all you need to make the transition from left to right brain, from mental distraction to mental quiet, from tension to relaxation.

Mental rehearsal: Walking yourself through every aspect of an impending performance demands total right-brain participation. Only your right brain has the sensory memory to furnish your rehearsal with all the appropriate detail that makes it seem real.

Music: Music has the power to totally transport us. If you need to be transported to a calmer, more ordered place, try playing classical music. Studies have found that baroque composers like Vivaldi, Bach, and Mozart use rhythms and constructs that induce alpha-wave brain states. On the other hand, if you need to psych yourself up or get the juices going, try listening to movie or Broadway sound tracks. They're scored to tell whole plot lines, sketch complete characters, and spell out emotional themes without a word. Make sure that you find some inspirational ones.

Symbols: Remember the musician who bought the Purple Heart to pin on her instrument case? Whether it's a medal, a framed diploma, a picture in your wallet, or an Emmy statuette, talismans of your achievements can routinely pack a wallop. Don't hide them. Put them where you can't help but see them before going into your next battle.

Sensual cues: For Anthony it was the silken feel of the scarf at his neck that reminded him of the flamboyant salesman he needed to be; for Steve it was the feeling of being sheathed head-to-toe in fireproof underwear that heated up his killer instinct. Dress for success. Wear something that makes you feel right for the job. Or carry something you can touch. (Maybe this explains why the rabbit's foot came to be associated with luck: All you have to do is touch it.)

Visualization: If your immediate environment doesn't delight your senses and refresh you, imagine a place that does—something from a vacation spot, something from your dreams, something from a movie or painting or play. It can be like taking a minivacation.

Humor: Humor can loosen you up, relax you, make you feel as though the stakes aren't life-and-death—because they very rarely are. Listen to comedians on your car stereo on the way to work. Read a page or two from a Dave Barry book. Run mental clips from movies or plays that made you howl. Or think of friends who crack you up.

(Whenever I'm about to lecture, I simply say to myself, "Tom Ness," and the memory of this funny guy I worked with at *Golf Digest* is enough to help me shed my whole overbearingly serious lecture tone. I can say his name, see him in my mind's eye, hear him, remember some of his stunts with the other golfers and pros, and step into his comic role.)

Now that you have all the tools you need to build total focus, it's time to put them all together. Turn to Appendix E for a three-week guide to reaching ultimate focus.

Ultimate Focus

There's a place, of course, for analysis, for deductive reasoning, for linear thought. The workplace rewards it. Corporate America prizes it. Technology wouldn't be possible without it. But our culture demands we spend a disproportionate amount of our waking lives at the jackhammer frequency of left-brain thinking. I say disproportionate because it's during our alpha states—the periods of contemplative calm we induce through ritualized action or repetitive physical exercise—that we get mentally quiet enough to become single-minded. Focused. In the moment. Totally "on."

When you are single-minded, your focus is so total, so consuming, you close the gap between intention and accomplishment. You become one with your intention, with the object of your focus. You actually merge with it; there is no perceptible boundary between your mind and the thing it beholds.

The mystics had a word for this experience: rapture.

It's such an awesome feeling, such a feeling of power, that given even a brush with it, you can't help but be willing to devote energy and discipline to getting more of it.

"People get discouraged because their mind is racing, and they have difficulty centering," Cal notes. "They get frustrated because they've never practiced slowing down that analytical left brain. But they need to keep at it. Because even if they have only five or six seconds of right-brain thought, it's worthwhile—it's probably more than they've had in the past ten years. A little makes a big difference!"

Cal can quantify the difference it's made for him. Whereas he used to go in to confer with his boss with his mind racing, now he stays right on the subject—and notices how distracted his boss is. He's more effective in day-to-day interaction, too. "When people feel like you're really concentrating on them, like they are totally your focus, they feel really listened to," Cal observes. "They'll come back to you. They'll want to do business with you. It's very powerful."

But it's in the presentations to the executive committee that Cal feels his perseverance has really paid off.

"It's an awesome feeling, to give a knockout presentation," he told me. "It's like that feeling I had when I was playing football, knowing, just knowing, where the running back was going to be, even before he got the ball.

"That's what total focus is about," he said. "Not thinking ahead. Not worrying about screwing up. Just being in the moment."

SUMMARY

The ability to focus—to train one's total attention on a person, conversation, or task—is in desperately short supply in our fast-paced culture. Yet while there's considerable attention paid to attention deficit disorder, there's very little written about how to reverse the trend. This chapter is perhaps the first and most comprehensive treatise on how to improve one's focus. Specifically, it addresses:

* Presence—the ability to stay in the moment
* Intensity—the ability to rally the energy that focus requires and train it like a laser on the task at hand
* Duration—the ability to sustain the intensity of one's focus

* Mental quiet—the ability to get past mental chatter and left-brain distraction

Exercises include how to:

* Get past external distraction
* Create attentional boundaries
* Get in the here and now through centering
* Allocate energy to conserve it for periods of intense focus
* Rally energy through centering up
* Modulate energy to optimal levels through visualization
* Sustain visual focus
* Sustain auditory focus
* Sustain kinesthetic focus
* Sustain focus under adverse conditions

The key strategy introduced in this chapter is the **pre-event routine**—a series of rituals that **move you out of distracting left-brain thinking** into the still pond of nonthinking known as **mental quiet**. Components of an effective pre-event routine include centering, mental rehearsal, music, symbols, sensual cues, visualization, and humor.

Remember, turn to Appendix E for your own Focus Plan.

CHAPTER SIX

Poise: How to Develop Ease in Decision Making, Negotiating, Presenting, and Multitasking

There is time enough for everything in the course of the day if you do but one thing at once; but there is not time enough in the year if you will do two things at a time.

—LORD CHESTERFIELD

Ed McMahon had a problem he needed to solve.

You may remember Ed. He's the guy whose goals we examined back in Chapter One—the senior manager of the equity trading group at Merrill Lynch. Ed wanted to make a difference—not just in how he did his job and lived his life but in how the 150 brokers, floor traders, and sales traders who worked for him did their job and lived their lives.

Merrill Lynch wanted him to make a difference too—in its bottom line. In 1998 and 1999 his group's revenues for the firm had grown by 20 percent each year. Could he sustain that rate of growth in 2000?

Two months into the year, Ed was looking at a 20 percent downturn in the "old economy" stocks his group traded—oil and gas, pharmaceuticals, and apparel—which were tanking as investors poured money into tech stocks and Internet IPOs. Day by day the S&P 500 graph each trader watched on his computer screen headed farther south.

"Every morning, I'd walk onto the trading floor, see the look on everybody's face, and think, *These people don't deserve this,* Ed recalled.

Then, in mid-March, the tech-heavy NASDAQ suffered a 30 percent "correction." Ed's stocks shot up as investors fled from fledgling Internet stocks to blue-chip heavyweights. Morale on the trading floor went up.

But so did the number of mistakes the traders made. Eager to make up for the previous three months, they either got out of positions prematurely or failed to bail out quickly enough. They were skittish. Prone to second-guessing themselves. Doubting of their instincts, forgetful of their training.

To get an extra 20 percent out of this group, Ed realized, he was going to need to retool. The volatility of the markets, the continued stress on their lives—if he pushed them any harder, he was going to see the thirty-year-olds crash and burn and the forty-five-year-olds take their money and run.

"My people model needed to change," he said. "My traders needed help internally. To do this job better throughout the day, a person needs to come in here with the right set of mind, ready to go, and then go home to his six-year-old feeling good about himself, whether the market's up or down five hundred points."

Merrill Lynch had sponsored corporate retreats for just this purpose. But while everybody came back from these gigs feeling up, Ed explained, the feeling didn't translate into a lasting coping strategy. "These off-site things are too *kumbayah,*" Ed had told the head of human resources. His people didn't need more feel-good inspiration thrown at them; they needed a set of tools to draw on every day.

"I didn't want to have a shrink come in here and change us into a bunch of tie-dye hippies," Ed added. "I can't afford to have my traders lose their edge. We want that drive, that energy. I just wanted someone to clarify, 'This is how to be more effective.' "

I started working with Ed and sixteen of his senior block traders in mid-March. Ed didn't look me up; he'd never heard of me. I had sought out Merrill Lynch as a testing ground for this program, much as I had sought out the SWAT trainees in order to test centering for my dissertation. I needed people having trouble performing under the relentless pressure of a high-stakes business environment—specifically, people having trouble making decisions, negotiating, making presentations, and multitasking. Ed needed someone to help out those of his people having trouble meeting the multiple demands of a big-capital trading floor.

Each of us believed we had made the other guy happen.

And each of us came away feeling we had indeed found the ideal solution to our problem.

What Is Poise?

Poise is how we describe those who perform with ease under fire. The term has been used to describe orators and athletes, leaders and statesmen, soldiers and surgeons. It is used to describe grace under pressure; the pressure itself can arise from just about any high-stakes situation.

But I use the term in this chapter with a specific set of pressures in mind. In the business world, no matter what the nature of the business, one's abilities are almost invariably put to the test in four, and only four, different performances. Those who succeed in business are those who consistently demonstrate the ability to remain determined, self-assured, in control, and focused when called upon to

* Make critical decisions
* Negotiate high-stakes deals
* Make presentations to a group of colleagues, superiors, or strangers
* Multitask, which I define as the ability to shift one's total focus from one task to another in rapid succession. (Effective multi-

tasking is *not* fracturing one's attention to focus on several things at once.)

You may well know how to arrive at a decision, or how to structure a talk, or how to strike a deal, but if you scored low in Poise, it's because you cannot consistently *act* on what you know. When you're *under pressure* to act decisively, speak persuasively, or deal like a poker player, your abilities desert you. This chapter will show you how to perform with ease and competence these four skills no matter how intense the scrutiny or time pressure, no matter how high the stakes or life-affecting the outcome.

It should be apparent that poise consists of all the factors in the success equation that we've addressed so far: determination, energy, perspective, courage, and focus. To have poise is to have all these qualities, plus the ability to make them work in concert with each other. Because *decision making, negotiating, presenting,* and *multitasking* under pressure are performances that demand an integrated strategy, this chapter will give you that strategy. It will show you how to mix and match the exercises discussed in previous chapters such that they add up to a whole greater than its parts. Even when the heat is cranked up to nuclear reactor levels, when it comes to performing these four business skills you will be:

* Energetic, but in control
* Confident, not self-absorbed with doubts and fears
* Attentionally in control—focused on the here and now
* At the top of your game, but relaxed enough to enjoy the performance

I would not presume to teach you, in the space of a chapter, how to make decisions, negotiate, or make presentations; these are skills that to some degree you must already possess. But I am going to give you new approaches—ones that will not fail you under stress—that combine tactics reviewed in previous chapters (centering, mental rehearsal, pre-event routine, process cues) with new ones I introduce here: how to be creative, how to mind-map, and how to achieve flexibility of attention. The key to poise—to performing optimally in decision making, negotiating, presenting, and multitasking under stress—is learning to rapidly shift to, and fully engage, the right brain. The exercises and strategies you'll find here will help you make the shift and apply your creative brain to situations conventionally thought to require analytical skills.

Poise in Multiple Performances

Athletes and stage performers need ease under pressure in only one skill, in only one performance: an Olympic competition, an audition for a seat in a major orchestra, a Grand Prix race, a U.S. Open golf tournament. Every business or sales executive, on the other hand, is called upon to perform in a series of events all day, every day.

My seventeen Wall Street traders, for instance, had to stay on top of forty-five industry groups—each might track as many as a hundred stocks—from the opening bell at 9:30 to the close of markets at 4:00. At any given moment, a trader would need to know what an individual stock was doing. He might make a hundred decisions in the course of a day, many in the blink of an eye. He might strike just as many deals. What price could he afford to pay a seller? At what price could he find a buyer? When was it time to load up? How many strategies had he thought out in the event he had to bail out of a position?

On every desk, in addition to the four screens and two news wires vying for their attention, the block traders had a couple of "squawk boxes" by which they communicated to other brokers—brokers on the Merrill Lynch floor, on the NYSE, and in forty-five retail offices across the country. It wasn't enough for a trader to know what his stocks were doing or how well his positions were faring; he also needed to communicate what he knew and what he believed to everybody else whose trade decisions depended on his. Part of a trader's job was to make these thirty-second presentations, even when he was so rattled by the markets or engulfed with information he couldn't remember his own name.

Nor were these communications limited to the phones and squawk boxes. Every Wednesday morning, all the senior equity traders met with seventy to eighty of their colleagues in the theaterlike conference room to report on their industry sectors and market strategy.

In sum, Ed's team had to excel at presentations, deal negotiations, and decision making—frequently all at the same time. Multitasking was the name of the game. It wasn't enough to be a star trader, to hit home runs on the desk every morning: You had to be good at pitching, catching, fielding, and base-running too.

"This is Yankee Stadium," Ed told me, as I gazed out over the 65,000 square feet of trading floor he oversees. "Except that it's the World Series here every day."

Making Better Decisions

We're accustomed to thinking at jackhammer frequency because we're constantly pressed to process information with our analytical mind. It's an occupational hazard of living in the information age. The left brain orders and sequences, analyzes and computes, evaluates and stores data. Like a computer, it processes all input in a linear fashion.

But the left brain is not much of a problem solver. It can't come up with new ideas; it's not creative. It can't see possibilities; it's not intuitive. It's not open to alternatives; it's absolutist, programmed to understand only ones and zeros, successes or failures, right and wrong. It refuses to suspend judgment until all the options are on the table; instead, it's constantly criticizing and evaluating. It cannot "think outside the box." It *is* the box.

It's a good place for information to gather. But it's a lousy place from which to make decisions on the information gathered. To make lightning-fast or life-affecting decisions without seizing up or blanking out or backpedaling, you must use your right brain, the intuitive, instinctive one. When it comes to seeing the big picture, only the right brain has the ability to pull away and apply some perspective. The right brain has the vision; it "sees" how all the bits of information come together. And the right brain is creative. Where the left brain is absolutist, insistent on only one correct answer, the right brain reflexively furnishes alternatives.

Too often, though, we don't make the shift from left brain to right brain before making a decision; we stay in the information-gathering hemisphere. Part of the problem is that many of us work in environments dominated by technology. At Merrill Lynch, for instance, computer screens outnumber humans five to one. Left-brain, computer-like thinking is prized—after all, there's an awful lot of information a trader must process if he's to keep pace with his markets.

But processing information is not what makes a trader good at trading. The decisions he makes regarding pricing and timing all depend on his "feel" for the markets—a sensibility no trader can put into words, because it arises from a place where words don't exist. "I just know when it's right," says Joey Mazzella, thirty-four, the senior trader who sits to Ed's right on the desk. "I always have a strong gut feeling."

Under extreme stress, the problem for guys like Joey is that they can't get in touch with their gut. They can't move into that right-brain mode which is so good at intuiting, sensing, and knowing in an instinctive way; they can't, because the left brain is in overdrive, analyzing, commenting, criticizing, second-guessing, filling their head with doubts, worries, fears, and irrelevant information. They can't *feel* anything because they can only *hear* what their left brain is telling them. When they try to make a decision on a trade, they "overeffort" it. They think too much.

When I started working with Joey, he was in a real batting slump. He was having trouble with his trade decisions because he was drowning in left-brain noise. Three months of rotten markets had shaken his confidence in his ability. He questioned whether he was even qualified for the job. He'd started on Wall Street fifteen years before as a runner; he'd never gone to college. Maybe he'd just been incredibly lucky to have come this far, he thought. Maybe the tremendous money he'd made the year before was just a fluke. But maybe his luck had run out. He didn't belong in this chair. He was a fraud, an impostor. Any day now his boss would get wise to him.

This kind of debilitating feedback is actually very common in people at the top of their field. One study of top-level execs showed "the impostor syndrome" afflicting more than half the group. It's the kind of self-talk that undermines confidence, poisons outlook, and stymies action. But it's easily remedied. The solution is to shift thinking from left to right hemispheres. That's best accomplished in two ways we've discussed in previous chapters: by centering and/or by devising a set of rituals, or pre-event routine, that moves you consistently into right-brain mode no matter how stressful the circumstances.

Centering to Get in Touch with Your Gut

At 9:15 every morning, Joey sits down, shuts his eyes, and gets clear. If somebody interrupts him, he starts over. If the left brain starts in with the impostor talk, he argues back. *Merrill Lynch pays me because I'm productive,* he counters. *I sit next to Ed because I give good advice to all the people who come looking for it. I may not have gone to college, but what I do every day isn't something learned in school. I have a God-given ability to make good decisions and be a profitable trader.*

"I know this," he says to himself out loud.

For Joey, centering gets the left-brain commentator—the nit-picking, anxious critic who keeps whispering *Fraud!*—to shut up. That allows him the mental stillness needed to check in with his gut, the place from which he makes trading decisions confidently and effectively.

THE PRE-DECISION ROUTINE

Centering may be enough of a pre-event routine to get you into right-brain mode. But other executives I've worked with are so left-brain—so accustomed to relying on their cognitive abilities—they need more of a ritual to effect the transition.

Paul*, fifty-seven, a venture capitalist I met on a Vail golf course, is one of these left-brainers. We worked on his golf game—not his decision making, at which he is very poised. Yet he insists that making a good decision is just like making a good shot from the fairway. You want to do all your computing—how much height or power you need, what kind of conditions you're up against, what club to use—*before* you step up to the ball, he says. He draws an imaginary circle around the ball, one with maybe a ten-foot radius. As long as he's standing outside of that circle, he's allowed to mull over all the technical considerations. But once he steps into it, that's his cue to stop thinking. "You can't nail the shot if you're still hearing last-minute instructions on how to hit it," he explains.

So, as in golf, Paul has come up with a routine he follows before deciding whether to back a company or bail out. He suspends judgment on a deal while he's in the information-gathering stage. As long as he's getting input from his people, as long as he's sitting in a conference room hearing all the pros and cons, he resists the temptation to arrive at any conclusions. Before he decides to invest or walk away from the deal, he walks away—literally—from the discussion.

"I'll get their input, but then I'll go off on my own," he explains. "You can process so much information you get bogged down in it to the point of losing sight of what the decision should be."

The conference room, in effect, is outside the ten-foot circle into which Paul steps when he wants to act decisively, not think about all the consequences. Even if he just steps into the hall, the bathroom, or his office, the important aspect of his routine is that he physically moves. And that cues his mind to move too—from the realm of discussion to the realm of resolution.

Negotiating Better Deals

The right brain is the place from which to negotiate as well, because negotiating is really nothing more than an interactive form of decision making.

Each party throws out information to be weighed and considered before both parties jointly arrive at a decision. If it's done right, both parties walk away feeling they have gained more than they have conceded.

Negotiation, like decision making, requires that you remain open-minded. You must remain aware of what you need while remaining cognizant of what the other party wants. This demands a certain amount of mental flexibility, in order to accommodate and adapt as the negotiation progresses. It won't progress at all if you enter it locked into a position. It will stop progressing the moment one party recognizes that the other has settled on a position and won't be open to further debate. You must suspend judgment until all options are on the table and all have been examined thoroughly. This takes a fair degree of self-control. To float ideas before judging them, you've got to be fairly grounded and self-assured. Emotions, fears, or doubts are poor judges to invite to sit in on the review process. When it comes time to narrow the range of options on the table, objectivity must be your only criterion.

But the key to successful negotiation is creativity. You can't meet each other in the middle if no one defines what the middle is. The definitions you both throw out for consideration are like stepping-stones: The more you lay on the table, the more easily both of you can move toward one another.

HOW TO GET CREATIVE

You may be able to throw out ideas in the heat of the negotiating. But your odds of performing optimally in that situation—your odds of being poised, that is—are much greater if you prepare for the event by brainstorming all the acceptable outcomes and all the ways by which you might arrive at them. Here are the ground rules that facilitate creativity.

1. Ideas flow most freely when you set time limits on the process. It's important to define the chunk of time in which you're going to let your brain storm. "I'm going to give this problem twenty minutes of my undivided attention in my office," or "I'm going to devote the morning to coming up with alternative terms to this deal," actually spurs idea flow, because you're putting limits on the duration of your concentration. Concentration can't be sustained indefinitely. Creativity requires you to put aside every other problem but that which you're trying to solve. If you allow your problem-solving session to be open-ended, other thoughts will perforce intrude. "Blue-sky thinking" flourishes when you impose durational and locational constraints on it.

2. Find or make the environment in which your thoughts flourish. Do you think more creatively with the blinds closed? With music playing? With white noise, such as an air conditioner, modulating the sound? People whose office environments don't permit much individual meddling often make their car the place for problem solving, and their commute the time frame in which they'll think of nothing else. Alternatively, you may have a conference room, a treadmill, or even a park bench that serves this purpose.

3. Adopt a routine for use in that environment. Maybe you get a cup of coffee before you settle in. Maybe you set up your phone so your calls go directly to voice mail. Maybe you just close your eyes. A set of rituals, as I've just reiterated, triggers the shift from left brain to right, from evaluative thinking to generative. Centering should be one of these rituals. Go back to our discussion in Chapter Six if you need help putting rituals together into a pre-event routine.

Now, let's say you're in your best idea environment, and you've cleared out the mental cobwebs. Your head is quiet; you've pushed away thoughts that don't pertain to the problem you'd like to solve, the decision you need to make, or the negotiation for which you need to come up with options. You're ready for the ideas to come, the solutions to appear, the options to take shape. How do you make them?

MIND MAPPING

1. **Take out a blank sheet of paper.** Don't use a legal pad or graph paper; the lines impose an order on what you write down, and it's way too premature for that. Trying to assign priority only gets in the way of coming up with material to prioritize.

2. **On the paper, draw a circle.** This circle represents the bubble we talked about in Chapter One—in which you put the outcome you most want. (Review Chapter One if you're hazy on how to fill in the bubble.) This is the goal. This is the vision. This is the mission you want most to accomplish. Never mind if it seems unrealistic—again, it's way too early to levy judgments like that. You're going to suspend that judgment for now.

3. **Outside the circle, anywhere on the paper, write down all the ideas that might get you what's in the bubble.** Fill up the paper or empty your head, whichever comes first.

4. **Circle them.**

5. **Now connect the circles according to how you perceive they relate to one another, and how ultimately they connect to the bubble.** What you see on the page will probably resemble a molecular structure.

In the course of this exercise, you may decide you need to change what's in the central bubble. Remember, as with goal mapping, you want to allow only what excites you as an outcome, only what you want most—not what you think others will make you settle for, not what you think you "should" put in there. Again:

Suspend judgment. No one is looking over your shoulder. No editor is waiting to pounce on you, unless it's the one who lives in your left brain—and you're keeping that one gagged and bound for the moment.

6. **Review what's on the page.** Take a moment to make sure you're centered. Check in with your gut as you examine the possibilities on the paper.

7. **Make a decision.** Take a highlighter and color the option(s) your gut likes the best.

This approach to problem solving is my adaptation of what's called *mind mapping*. It is the brainchild of Michael Gelb, whose audiotape series *Mind Mapping: How to Liberate Your Natural Genius* is worth a look. The technique has enormous application in any kind of complex decision making or systems analysis, where there isn't one right answer but rather many acceptable compromises. It's a neat way to get around the black-and-white, pass-fail, absolutist thinking that asserts itself most unwelcomely when the pressure's on. It's a great way to come up with what you want to communicate most in a negotiation, because it furnishes you so many solutions, you cannot fail.

And it's the best way I know of to keep your mind open and flexible—to resist saying no right off the bat, or otherwise communicating that you're not going to play ball, because that attitude is what makes a negotiation fail. It communicates you're afraid. Poise in negotiation is radiating a combination of open-mindedness, self-assurance, and a willingness to push the envelope.

Mike*, another of the senior traders, felt he was a natural negotiator—and every trade, he pointed out, is a negotiation. Trades were second nature to him. He arrived at a price or an amount by instinct. But every now and then, he explained, a deal would involve enough risk to make him nervous. When he was nervous, he admitted, he tended to be negative. Instead of focusing on the possibilities, he could only focus on the thing turning sour. Reflexively, he'd say no to whatever the seller proposed.

Mind mapping, however, gave him a plan—a way to handle the riskier deals in a positive, proactive way rather than his customary negative, reactive way. In the circle, he'd write down what the seller had in mind. Then he'd write down and circle two or three ways he could handle the deal. He drew lines from those circles to ideas on how each scenario might play out. With practice, Mike found, he didn't even need the paper: He could "see" the ideas and the scenarios in his head. He'd review the possibilities with his gut, and rank them, mentally, in order of likely success.

In a recent bid for a stock, Mike stated the price he could pay and the amount he wanted. The seller came back and said no—he was looking to get more done, at a different price. "My initial reaction," Mike said, "was to just stick with my original bid. Be rigid. But then I drew the circle, came up with a couple different ways to handle the deal, and picked the one I thought had the most upside. I fought off my knee-jerk reaction. I changed my price and amount."

Mike's process cue, interestingly enough, is simply "yes."

And the deal worked out. "We got a higher price for the seller than we'd talked about, and we got another customer to buy it, so we got commissions on both sides of the deal," Mike adds. "It was a win-win situation."

So to review:

1. Write down the problem you need to solve, the decision you need to make, or the goal you want to arrive at in a deal.
2. Center and/or go through your pre-event routine to shift from left brain to right brain.
3. In this frame of mind, consider the possibilities. Generate as many as you can. Say yes, for now, to all of them.
4. When you've got at least five, open your eyes and capture

them on paper. Resist making judgments until you've got
them all down.

5. Now check in with your gut. Circle those that appeal to
your instincts.

6. Choose one. Act on your decision.

Making Better Presentations

Negotiations and presentations have a lot in common: Half the battle
is in knowing what to say; the other half is in knowing how to say it.

Making a presentation with poise draws on all the skills I've discussed so far in this book. It requires determination; you need to know
what you want to accomplish, what message you want your audience
to leave with. It requires energy, modulated to the level at which you
perform best. It requires self-confidence. It takes guts. And it demands
you know how to focus, not just on your topic but on the delivery of
it to each person in the room.

In this chapter we've reviewed exercises mentioned in earlier chapters but with special emphasis on how they can be applied in select
pressure situations. I've also showed you how to maximize your creativity and organize it with mind mapping. Now let me show you how
these exercises can give you poise in making presentations.

Centering to Power Delivery

Most people confronted with a podium and a roomful of people
find their energy at explosive levels; they need to center down. But
once that energy's harnessed, they can use it to their advantage. One,
they can use it to project their voice and energize their tone. Instead
of sounding quiet or quavery, they come off as excited and colorful.
And two, they can use it to project confidence and optimism.

The usefulness of this second point isn't to be underestimated.
Every Wednesday morning, when the traders congregate in the conference room, Ed addresses them first—after he's taken a minute to

center, because he's realized it's not what he says so much as what his face, his hands, and his tone communicate. "If my face or tone says we're going to crash into a wall," he observes, "then they go out there and crash. Whereas if I'm positive and 'can-do,' that positive energy translates from me to them. The way I feel going into the presentation can dictate the flow of business for the day or even the week."

Mind Mapping to Structure a Speech

Getting your ideas down on paper as I showed you earlier—with bubbles you connect instead of an outline or list—helps structure a presentation in a way that makes it not only easier to deliver but more fun for your audience to listen to. And the more fun they have, the better they'll remember what you said.

Ed, who's a very visually oriented guy, was struggling to come up with a speech for his brother's fortieth-birthday party. There was so much he could say that he didn't know where to begin. "I don't know what structure to put on the thing," he lamented.

I got him to center. With his eyes still closed, I asked him to come up with three pictures, images taken from the past he shared with his brother.

Ed came up with more than three. Lots of pictures popped into his mind. Each picture told a story.

Great, I said. But remember that bubble: It'll break if you stuff too much into it. Choose three. The three you feel the most strongly about.

When he opened his eyes, I had him project those three images onto a piece of blank paper. He made three circles, each one with a few words to describe the visual, such as "awful yellow cake" and "Super Bowl commercial."

During your speech, I said, picture these circles, one at a time. Describe the first image to your audience as you see it in your mind's eye. Make them see the story you're telling. Then move to the next.

Ed took the process one step further. He brought along props to illustrate the images in his stories—an ugly yellow cake was one—and they got his audience laughing, which in turn got Ed even more comfortable in his storytelling. He wrapped his speech with an image he took from a television commercial, one where the camera asks the quarterback, after the Super Bowl, where he wants to go, and the quarterback responds, "Disney World." While he had the audience involved in this visual, Ed presented his brother with an envelope of vouchers for an all-expense-paid trip to Disney World.

"It felt great," says Ed. "I was the only one who spoke, but it didn't rattle me. I had a lot of strangers come up to me afterward and say, 'That was wonderful.' "

Directing Your Focus

In a negotiation, you are making a presentation to one person. That's generally easier than making it to five, or fifty, or five hundred people, because it's more like a normal conversation, the kind you have every day, one-on-one. Hence the trick to staying poised while presenting is to keep your focus under control. You want to stay focused on your theme—and the mind mapping, with its emphasis on distinct images, certainly helps. But you also want to stay focused on one person at a time. You want to train your exclusive attention on that person in a brief, intense burst—say, five seconds. After five seconds, move your laser beam to another person, moving around the room this way until you've covered every corner. Then start over, if you're not done. What you absolutely don't want to do is scatter your attention over the room like bird shot or dart your gaze around like a caged animal. This communicates you're afraid. Your audience picks up on that scent like a dog. They feel uncomfortable. They radiate their discomfort back to you. And that just makes you even more afraid and discombobulated.

To reiterate: Tell your story, or paint your pictures, to one person at a time, five seconds at a time, shifting your focus from person to person in a controlled way. More than anything else, this display of focus puts your audience at ease and you in the driver's seat. It feels like an intimate conversation to everyone in the room, including you. It's engaging. Neither you nor your audience will have a chance to drift off.

Act Out Your Stories

Words, as I said way back in the chapter on courage, are not enough: *Action* wins the day. Paradoxically enough, a poised speaker is one who feels relaxed enough, uninhibited enough, to indulge in physical expression.

Let your body act on what your mind sees. If you're describing going over a waterfall in a kayak, let your whole body express the experience and illustrate the image. Props can help encourage this response. It's easier to act when a prop gives you reason to.

This is not to say *any* action is appropriate. Pacing, bobbing up and down, clenching your fists, tapping your fingers, or otherwise expressing your nerves is very distracting and sends, again, the message that you're afraid or not in control. Don't move unless the movements help you paint a picture, illustrate a concept, or demonstrate an action.

Staying in the Here and Now

This gets back to what we termed "presence" in the chapter on focus. Allow yourself to get caught up in what you're saying, in the visuals or feelings you're sharing, in the action you're demonstrating, and you won't lose yourself or your audience.

It's especially important to stay in the here and now when answering questions. *Really listen,* with your full attention, to what's being asked, instead of rushing to abort the question with an answer. You can buy yourself time to formulate an answer by repeating the question back to the audience. If the question is hostile, state it in a less hostile way, one you can answer without having to rise to the bait.

Pulling It All Together: A Poised Presentation

The more in-the-moment you are, the more your audience feels the embrace of your whole attention. The more focused you are in your gaze, the more intimate the contact you establish. The more vivid or visceral the images you describe, and the more expressive your body language becomes, the less likely your audience will find something more exciting to think about. The more open-minded your attitude to their questions, the more interested they'll be in your response—and the more questions they'll want to ask you.

In short, they'll be enthralled. And you'll feel it. Rather than wishing you could dissolve into the floor or disappear behind the podium, you'll wish the experience could last a little longer.

That's how A. C. Morgan felt when he spoke to about sixty M.B.A. students at Syracuse University.

A.C., thirty, another member of Ed's trading team, wasn't uncomfortable speaking in public. He had a tendency, however, to spray his eye contact around a room like a machine gun.

"If I get overwhelmed by the crowd, I can't make individual contact," he admitted. "Then my audience doesn't feel like they're a part of it. The more I sense them drifting away, the more nervous I get, and the whole thing starts spinning out of control. I start saying, 'ah' and 'um' and 'y' know.' The crowd loses confidence in me. And then I lose confidence in myself."

At Syracuse, however, A.C. got the feedback loop to spiral upward, not down. He centered before he went in. The breathing, he said, got him focused; the mental quiet allowed him to tune out the voices of doubt and feel confident. To get his audience involved, he structured his talk as a "multi-way" conversation, throwing out questions and inviting people to respond.

Immediately, that changed the dynamic. A.C. felt at ease because the responsibility for the talk didn't all rest on him. He used his hands and arms, gesturing, laughing, and his audience laughed with him. Hands shot up with questions. A.C. took his time answering them. The audience took his pauses to mean he was in control.

"The confidence I had going in," says A.C., "they radiated back to me. The whole thing just spun higher and higher. I had to cut short the Q and A. When that happens, you know you did a good job."

PRESENTATION PRACTICE

If you want to do a good job at your next presentation, here are the points to keep in mind:

* Mind-map to come up with several stories with strong visuals.
* Mentally rehearse telling those stories.
* Practice your gesturing and storytelling in front of a mirror or video camera. Remember, you want your gestures to depict actions and express your feelings.
* Gather a few friends or colleagues and do a dry run.
* Speak to each of them, one at a time, for five seconds.
* Use any energy you feel to power your voice and express your enthusiasm.
* Smile.

By the way, trial presentations count as courageous entries in your Courage Log.

Multitasking More Effectively

By now, it should be pretty clear how essential it is to center, get mentally quiet, be creative, and focus in order to be a more poised decision maker, negotiator, and presenter. But I have one more case to make for the application of these skills, and that's in applying them to those situations in which we're called upon to multitask—to juggle several performances at once. Multitasking especially relies on the ability to focus; poise in multitasking is a function of making rapid shifts of total concentration.

Juggling is certainly Joey Mazzella's most challenging performance. All day long, but especially in the morning, when the markets are at full throttle and he's trying to put on trades for the day, people come to him for advice or input because they can't get to his boss. Meanwhile, traders scream numbers at him from across the room. Every couple of minutes Joey answers the phone, makes a call, or does a broadcast over the squawk box.

As one of the senior guys on the desk, and especially as the guy who sits next to Ed, he's supposed to field crises, answer questions, and give advice. He's also supposed to think out loud, frequently, on the squawk box or phone. But he's also expected to trade in three different industries. And after turning his attention from the phone or the box or the person tapping him for advice, Joey finds it hard to get back into the thought process of trying to place a trade. So his strategy, often, is to keep his mind on the trade while giving only some of his attention to what he's saying over the squawk box, what he's saying or hearing on the phone, or what he's being told by someone.

"I'm watching a sales trader's lips move, I'm smiling and nodding, I'm letting him express himself," says Joey, "but I'm not really listening, because I've heard it a hundred times before, and I've got a position to think about."

To Joey's way of thinking, this is multitasking. But it isn't, because it isn't working. Everything that gets a fraction of his attention gets only fractionally resolved. "People sense when they're not getting your full attention," I pointed out. "They don't feel satisfied, so they come back. Then they wind up taking even more of your time."

Even Joey conceded, "I'm so jittery, half the time I sound like an idiot on the squawk box. I can't slow my mouth because I can't slow my brain."

Multitasking is not, as most people seem to think, the application of your divided attention to many things at once. It's not a spray of bird shot. It's just the opposite: It's a rapid shift of your total attention. You concentrate intensely on one thing at a time, but because you shift that concentration so quickly and effortlessly from one thing to another, it appears that you're handling them all simultaneously. Multitasking is having a flexibility of total focus. It's sharpshooting.

But first you've got to have total focus.

Assess Your Concentration

As I discussed in the chapter on Focus, what gets in the way of total concentration is often not the outer noise, but the inner—the negative self talk, the doubts about ability, the fears of inadequacy or failure. As I showed the senior traders, this left-brain noise severely detracts from their ability to use the few seconds they have to attend fully to one task before they cross it off and move to the next.

I gave several of the traders a little test you can try yourself. In the grid you see below, numbers appear in random sequence. I told them to find the next higher number after 00, cross it off, and move on. I gave them sixty seconds to cross off as many numbers as possible in order. Then I had them write down all the things they were thinking or feeling as they tried to race through the test.

The ones who scored well had nothing to write down. "Whaddya mean, what was I thinking?" one guy said. "I was taking the test!"

Whereas the ones who scored poorly were thinking about a lot—everything, apparently, but looking for the next number. They noticed me watching them. They wondered if they should skip numbers. They worried about their scores. They heard, "Hurry up! What's

26	75	18	63	42	82	05	30	47
08	03	73	80	57	17	76	51	13
33	25	28	12	84	89	40	66	20
10	43	37	45	90	27	86	35	69
55	49	21	70	22	88	02	64	54
39	34	65	81	44	61	87	15	59
58	01	78	31	14	48	85	72	07
41	38	52	56	36	83	74	79	60
23	06	68	77	19	71	24	09	29
11	46	62	32	50	04	53	16	67

wrong with you? Can't you move any faster than that? You're not going fast enough!"

That left-brain monkey doesn't make you go any faster, I pointed out to the low scorers. It just gets in the way of what you're doing.

See for yourself: Take the concentration test on page 165. Have someone time you for sixty seconds. When you're done, give yourself a point for each number you marked. Then write down all the instructions, criticisms, comments, or noise your left brain made while you were trying to sequence the numbers.

Now take a look at what you've written. There's usually a strong correlation between the number of things you wrote down and your score: the longer your list, the fewer numbers you managed to cross off.

But you can change that.

The point of the exercise is not to see how many numbers you can cross off: It's simply to reveal the monkey on your back, pressing you to hurry up—as though this kind of pressure will actually help. It doesn't. You've got to shake off this monkey. Until you do, your multitasking ability will be compromised, because your concentration is impaired.

Getting the Monkey Off Your Back

How to shake him? The first step: Becoming aware, simply, that he's there.

Some years ago I was asked to attend a U.S. Swimming National Team training camp in Hawaii. This ten-day event gathered the best swimmers and the best coaches in the country to work on ways to shave just a few more milliseconds off their times. I was asked by the coaches to help on one particular problem: getting the swimmers off the blocks faster. At the sound of the starting gun, a top athlete could literally blow his race if he suffered so much as a fractional delay in response. Or, he'd have to swim that much harder over the next 100 meters to compensate for his "slow" start.

I got the swimmers on the pool deck and had them assume a starting position—with their arms down at their sides, and slightly crouched, ready to jump. Then I fired the gun and had them timed in their response. "What were you thinking," I asked them, "between the sound of the gun and your jump?"

For the fractionally slower ones, it was something like: "Ohmigod there's the gun get moving you're already behind oh shit you've lost precious time they're already way ahead of you . . ."

Such thoughts took only a few milliseconds. And yet, the swimmers could see that even a millisecond of thought was costing them. Some of them had bought into the idea that they simply weren't good at getting off the blocks—as though there were some physical reason. But they quickly recognized that the delay was purely mental. It was that monkey holding them up.

With that new awareness, they were able to put a stop to the thinking. They became one with the sound of the gun: All of their attention was in the nerve cells of their ears. I shot off the gun maybe two more times and timed them. The stopwatch proved it, but you could see it: There was no more delay.

The grid test you took a few moments ago is one way to spark this awareness and help you react faster by shaking that monkey off your back. But look beyond this little test to others you take, perhaps unwittingly, every day. Ask yourself: *Am I making this worse for myself? Does the goading*—"Hurry up!" or "You don't have much time!" or "Can't you do better?"—*help me do better?*

Definitely not.

You can silence the goading voice, believe it or not, by simply saying, "Shut up." But I like even better an affirmative put-down: Say, instead, "I'm doing the best I can." Keep saying it, until it becomes almost a mantra: *I'm doing the best I can.* After a while, you won't even have to say it. You'll know it. The monkey pressuring you will know it. He'll back off and shut up.

A slight variation on this tactic is what I got Joey to do whenever his particular monkey hissed, "You have no idea what you're doing!" He'd refute it. He'd offer all the arguments, all the evidence, that proved he *did* know his job—quite well, in fact. Until finally, all Joey needed to say to himself was "I know this." It was an affirmation, not a defense. It silenced the chimp.

Internal thoughts and words interfere with total concentration, which in turn interferes with your ability to zero in on a task, get it done well, and move on to the next. Getting rid of that interference is clearly the first step in learning to multitask. You may, however, suffer from other interference: You may need to work on lengthening your attention span and shutting out all external distraction as well. I suggest you reread or review Chapter Five for a complete strategy on improving your focus. At the very least, practice Centering (the focus of Chapter Two), as I had Joey do every morning, just so you have the mental quiet to be *aware* of the monkey and then shrug him off.

Using Process Cues to Speed Shifts of Focus

Once you've got the ability to concentrate, it's time to learn how to shift, rapidly, your full attention from one thing to another. Making these shifts is the essence of multitasking.

The key to shifting is coming up with an effective process cue, the sort of trigger we discussed in Chapter Two. A good process cue works in two ways: It acts as a mental trigger, one designed to click you into right-brain mode instantaneously. And it can be used to trigger instantaneous shifts in your attention, from one task or focus to another.

Let's review what makes a good process cue.

1. **A word or phrase which summons an image, sound, or sensation.** Maybe you find a word to describe a quality you aspire to have, such as "assured," or "smooth." These "concept" words work as long as you can picture or hear or feel that quality when you say the word to yourself.

2. **Someone's name—someone who embodies the attributes you admire.**

3. **A mental snapshot or actual picture of the person, place, or

thing that represents the qualities or frame of mind you're seek-
ing. Maybe you see someone's face; maybe you see a serene place, like
a waterfall in a wooded glade.

4. A word that summons an entire memory of you performing
(multitasking) especially well. Perhaps by saying "PTA" you instantly recall a time when you ran a fund raiser and managed many
tasks especially well.

5. An actual sensation, one that hooks you into performing an
action without having to think of your action in words. A skier I
worked with had only to "feel" her big toe against the inside of her
boot to trigger the series of movements necessary to execute a good
turn. In multitasking situations, maybe you actually stroke something
smooth, like a pebble, to trigger smooth attentional transitions.

Once you've got a process cue you like, take the concentration test
again. (Have someone make you a new grid, with numbers in different places.) Every time a distracting thought tries to intervene, summon your process cue to get back into your right brain. If the one
you've chosen doesn't seem to help your score improve, try another
one.

Selecting Process Cues for Speed Shifts

The most effective process cues are nonverbal, because nothing
cues the right brain faster than a non-left-brain stimulus. When it
comes to multitasking—making what I call "speed shifts" of your total concentration from one task to another—nonverbal process cues
such as images, sounds, and sensations can make you a masterful mul-
titasker.

Yet I've found that most of my clients arrive at these nonverbal
cues usually only after they get the hang of using verbal ones. For instance, one woman chose the word "juggling," which is a pretty left-
brain way to describe a very right-brain activity. Eventually, however,
she just flashed in her mind a mental snapshot of an actual circus performer keeping dozens of plates spinning simultaneously. The picture

became her process cue whenever she was called upon to juggle tasks. Similarly, Joey started out with the words "olive oil," but it was the kinesthetic properties of olive oil that wound up helping him make rapid attentional shifts. He imagined the way it felt, the slipperyness, the smoothness. These imagined sensations worked much quicker and more effectively than the actual words.

Process cues which help you speed shift your attention are, understandably, images, sensations, and sounds having to do with speed. Bill, the voiceover guy in Chapter Five, often had to do a commercial in a very short time frame. He needed to get pumped up, yet he needed to concentrate in order to deliver the enunciation his employers wanted. Bill imagined, as his process cue, the sound of a train passing him on the platform: He could hear and *feel* the speed of the oncoming train. Instantly, he was able to shift into high-energy, high-speed mode himself.

Having worked with Grand Prix drivers, all I need to do to get in that mode is hear in my head the unforgettable ripping, screaming, roar of a Formula race car zipping by. It could be the press of air that walloped me—the sensation of speed that gust of air communicated. Similarly, I have felt that sense of power and speed in my gut whenever I'm sitting in a jet accelerating down the runway.

The point is to figure out what does it for you: What sensation of speed, or sound of speed, or image of speed can you make your process cue for mutitasking situations? It may not be a sound; it may be a musical theme, or beat. (The song "Danger Zone" from *Top Gun* always works for me: I just need to hear the lead guitar part and I'm fired up.)

When you hit upon the image, sound, or sensation that revs you, put it to the test. Find a multitasking situation and practice triggering rapid attentional shifts with your process cue.

Every weekday Joey puts his to the test. When the markets open at 9:30 and the room starts to buzz, Joey is centered and ready to field all the balls hurled at him. Nine people may be screaming at him, his markets may be tanking, but he's staying in the moment, shifting his attention from one task to the next, making decisions, hearing out the sales trader, processing the information on his screens, or presenting new information over the squawk box. He's multitasking with poise.

And he can see the difference. He can measure it. Two weeks into his new regimen, Joey made 40 percent of the entire group's weekly profit. It was his biggest week ever.

"Maybe this stuff is psychosomatic," he says. "But so what? It works. I don't get tight. I don't feel the self-doubt. I get the clarity I need. And when I get that gut feeling, I know not to second guess it. That's why I had such a good week."

Summary

Poise is how we describe those who consistently demonstrate the ability to remain determined, self-assured, in control, and focused when called upon to

* Make critical decisions
* Negotiate high-stakes deals
* Make presentations to a group of colleagues, superiors, or strangers
* Multitask, or shift one's total focus from one task to another in rapid succession

To perform these four skills under stress requires a new approach, one which applies tactics from previous chapters (centering, mental rehearsal, pre-event routine, process cues) in conjunction with how to be creative, how to mind-map, how to shake the left-brain monkey off your back, and how to select process cues to speed shifts in your attention.

Appendix F is a simple chart that allows you to build and strengthen all four skills over twenty-one days.

And remember, poise is invariably a function of applying your creative brain to situations conventionally thought to require analytical skills. The secret to making decisioins, negotiating, making presentations, and multitasking is to "right-brain it."

Turn to Appendix F for your own Poise Plan.

CHAPTER SEVEN

Resilience: How to Recover from a Mistake or Setback

*Inside the ring or out, ain't nothing wrong with going
down. It's staying down that's wrong.*

—MUHAMMAD ALI

Remember the speed skater Dan Jansen? You may recall the last race
of his career, in Lillehammer, Norway, during the 1994 Winter
Olympic Games. The pressure on him to win could not have been
greater. He'd been to three Olympics, and despite proving himself a
world champion in every other international contest, he had yet to
stand on that uppermost platform and receive the gold medal.

Yet within seconds of the starting gun going off, Dan made a mistake. His skate nicked the lane divider. He reached down to touch the
ice to steady himself. A collective gasp went up from the crowd.

"That'll cost him," the announcers told us grimly.

But it didn't. Dan not only won that race but set a world record in the process—and took home, at long last, the gold.

The mistake didn't cost him a victory because he didn't allow it. In the fraction of an instant his finger touched the ice, he made a decision. He decided not to react. He decided not to indulge the reflex that causes lesser athletes to lose their focus and obsess over the consequences of what's already beyond their control. That obsession, not the mistake itself, is what ultimately costs them the outcome they covet.

Essentially, Dan didn't give his left brain a chance to weigh in. He didn't give the critical commentator even a fraction of a second to break his concentration with irrelevant observations about what just happened. He chose to stay in the absolute moment of what he was doing, which was skating at record speed.

The ability to move on—to put a poor judgment, a wrong answer, a weak moment, a physical lapse, behind you instantly—is the thing that makes winners out of the merely talented. Winners are not perfect. But they excel at damage control. They fight for what they want, no matter what comes between them and their goal; they continue to move forward. It's a skill they have cultivated above all others. Their talent may be inborn, but what distinguishes them from the competition, what time and again helps them snatch victory from the jaws of defeat, is this ability to escape the clutches of a mistake.

It's a skill I call resilience. And it's one you'll learn to cultivate in this chapter.

What Is Resilience?

Resilience, the final factor in the success equation, consists of three qualities or skills:

* The *ability to recover,* quickly, from a mistake, and not bog down in anger

- The *ability to fight* for what you most want or what you believe in, especially when the chips are down or the odds seem stacked against you
- *Mental toughness,* the ability to hang tough, mentally, no matter what assault is made on your confidence, no matter what setback you've suffered, no matter how late in the game you commit to winning it

The key to being resilient is understanding that *you can choose not to succumb to error, setback, or failure.* So much of what we presume to be involuntary is really within our control, as I have shown you from the beginning. We can choose not to allow stress to debilitate us; we can change our stress response. So, too, can we change our response to a screwup: We can choose not to bog down in anger or remorse. Resilience is a function of getting past those two emotions.

Choosing to move on is easier when we're armed and ready to deal with the inevitable—mistakes, that is. We'll start with a basic five-step recovery strategy. Then we'll look at getting past anger as a distraction; using anger to focus; and harnessing it to power a rebound. You'll see how it can work in golf, squash, and corporate politics.

As for fighting back, my strategy is to inspire you with tales of people who've done just that. Each found the fighter within and learned how to invite that fighter out when the moment called for it. We also worked on hanging in, because no fight is over in just one round. And I'll share with you the Principles of War—a list of instructions my civilian clients have found handy when about to head into everyday battles.

Finally, I'll prove to you that it's never too late to recover from a major setback. It's a matter of true grit, of mental toughness, coupled with a willingness to let go of perfectionism. It takes some heavy-duty self-talk work. But it can be done; I'll let you hear from someone who's made the journey.

Let's begin, however, by discussing how to recover from a mistake, because if you can do that, you can forestall a major setback. Failure is often simply the result of an error that was allowed to compound.

Developing the Ability to Recover

Think how you react in a restaurant when a waiter drops his tray. At the moment of impact, you swivel around in your chair to see the source of the crash. Everybody does. The sound of shattering china and cutlery commands attention. You feel you have no choice but to turn your gaze. There isn't time *not* to turn; before you're even conscious of what's happened, you're staring at the unfortunate waiter.

But in that nanosecond there *is* time. There's time to decide not to react. There's time to choose between staying in the moment, which is to say, ignoring the waiter and continuing to eat, and allowing your attention to dwell on what's already past, what's already irrelevant, what cannot be undone.

Making this choice takes practice. It takes energy. It takes will. It takes awareness.

Yet if you put the time and energy into practicing control over this type of reflex, you will have at your disposal a powerful tool for minimizing the impact of any mistake you make. That's how mistakes domino into disasters: They wrench our attention away from the present, from what we're doing, from what we can still control. Control the reflex, and it's almost as though the mistake never happened. You can recover. Instantly.

Learning this control is a process, one I've found can be boiled down to five steps. As with centering, these steps are going to look awfully complicated or lengthy at first. But as with centering, you'll find that with practice you can implement this recovery strategy in a matter of seconds. Even nanoseconds. And you'll get lots and lots of practice, because mistakes are a natural resource we never run out of.

FIVE-STEP RECOVERY STRATEGY

1. **Accept the mistake.** If you've ever played golf or tennis, you know just how much time you can waste in denial.

"I can't believe I missed that putt!"

"I never miss that shot! That's my best shot!"

"How can that have hit the net? That was a perfect serve!"

And so on. You say these dumb things because they help you vent—or you think they help you. But in fact, they only serve to give the mistake a toxic half-life it doesn't deserve. They lengthen the moment of disaster. They force you to interrupt your right-brain concentration with a word from your critical commentator, the left-brain one, which is always watching and waiting for a chance to get a word in edgewise—and seize control. Have you ever started to make an argument convincingly to a cohort and suddenly lost the thread because your left brain said, "You forgot your best point! How could you have left that out"? Let the left brain speak up, and you lose all right-brain ease of execution. Let the left brain get its two cents in, and you lose that priceless state of mind that allows you to just do your thing effortlessly.

Accept the mistake. That means you resist the temptation to acknowledge it in words. Don't let your left brain say a word, either in your head or out loud. What's done is done. Even one offhand comment can only make it worse.

You can accept a mistake even faster and more easily if you understand at the outset of your performance that you may make an error or two and that's okay. Mistakes are okay because they mean you're committed to giving your all, to holding nothing back. You're not going to play it safe, because no great performance ever came from holding back. Perfection is not only unrealistic, it's not what makes you great. If you commit to go for it, you commit to succeed no matter what goes wrong. You accept the fact that something might. Then you can practice your recovery strategy.

2. **Focus on the here and now.** The major damage from a mistake results from its power to steal you from the present. It steals your focus from what you're doing. Say you open your talk on a

breakthrough product with a joke, and the joke doesn't fly the way you expected. Every five minutes you remember that awkward opening moment, as though by reviewing it you can fix it—when in fact, every minute you review it steals from your ability to pitch the new product wholeheartedly. It's a lose-lose situation now, because focusing on what's past—the joke—can't change anything, while not focusing on what's present—the product pitch—can change the entire outcome of the presentation.

It's critical for you to develop presence, or the ability to focus beyond any distraction that might pull you out of the here and now. If you haven't mastered this, go back to Chapter Five. Only by focusing on what you're doing in the present moment can you actually affect outcome. Let go of the past no matter what you just failed to do and get your mind in the present on the task at hand.

3. **Relax the muscles** that reflexively tighten in response to making the mistake. Opera singers who miss a note find their throats constricting; golfers who miss a putt miss the next one because their arms or shoulders tense. Not everyone, of course, relies on muscles to perform, but all of us can do our job better if we can fend off the tension a mistake triggers.

Do this by first identifying which muscle group is most consistently affected by stress. Do you contract your shoulder muscles? Do you clench your teeth or your fists? Do you tighten chest muscles, so that your breathing becomes shallow? Use the centering technique discussed in Chapter Two to locate and de-stress the muscles that are prone to contract under performance pressure. With practice, relaxing these muscle groups will take no more than a second of conscious effort.

4. **Use your process cue** to remind yourself of what you need to do. Use it to get back into right-brain mode.

A mistake prompts your left brain to leap from the wings, where it's always waiting, onto center stage, where it loves to deliver its monologues. But don't let it, because your left brain is a critic, not a performer. Your right brain is the star performer, your right brain will yield the stage, however, unless you prompt it to go on. The process cue is that prompt. It speaks only to the right brain; it helps the right brain remember what to do. Without that process cue, the left brain behaves like the show is over and it's time to come on and criticize. It's not time. Keep the critic off stage until it's over—and it ain't over till the fat lady sings or you hear the audience clap. Bear in mind that your left-brain critic will have the rest of your life to analyze this performance; it would be a tragedy to allow it to stop the show before it's anywhere near over.

To encourage your star to carry on, you may need to repeat your process cue like a mantra, over and over. (If you need to review what makes a good process cue, turn to page 56.) Don't stop. The show must go on.

5. **Do it good before you try to do it great.** The tendency when recovering from a mistake is to try to make up for it with something stupendous. Watch minor league batters who strike out at the beginning of the game: The next time they're up at bat, they swing like maniacs, because they're hoping to erase their earlier performance with a homer. That only causes them to strike out again.

After you've struck out several times, what you need is a base hit. Get on base first, and your chances of a grand slam later in the game improve exponentially. You've got to get back on track before you can hope to make up for lost time.

That's the five-step recovery strategy. The more often you apply it, the quicker you'll get at it—until, like Dan in his Olympic heat, you'll be able to deploy it in a second or less.

Getting Past Anger

One of the block traders I worked with at Merrill Lynch, a guy we'll call Barry*, had great difficulty letting go of a mistake—not so much on the trading desk as on the squash court, where he was even more of a competitor. At work, Barry kept his cool; according to him, he was "one of the more laid-back guys on the desk." But get him out on the squash court, where he played almost nightly, and one poorly executed shot would undo him.

What were you thinking? You're such an idiot.
You suck!
How could you miss that? You're playing like shit.

These tirades weren't conducted only in his brain. A lot of the cursing, and certainly the tone, could be picked up by whomever he was competing against. Barry threw his racket. Smashed the wall with his fist. Stomped around the court.

"I was like McEnroe," he noted. "Not that I thought my shitty behavior was okay—I knew it wasn't. But I thought it wasn't correctable. I even told myself that it fired me up, like McEnroe, to play better."

Yet nothing was further from the truth. With every mistake Barry made, his anger ballooned and his performance spiraled downward. At one point his brother, a former pro tennis player, put it to him. "You look like a complete ass out there," he told Barry. "And it doesn't help you on the court."

Anger over a mistake is probably the number one reason mistakes get the better of us. We can't move on because we're in the thrall of our disappointment, our disgust at having screwed up. We feel the need to beat ourselves up for it—as though we won't learn from the mistake otherwise. So we invite the left brain to have a field day, because flogging is a left-brain specialty. We unleash on ourselves the sort of punishing talk we wouldn't dare use on a friend or colleague.

Somewhere in our subconscious we know *why* we wouldn't dare use it on a colleague. It's not just politically incorrect, it's completely unconstructive. It doesn't bring out a better performance: just the opposite.

But we can't stop. Or rather, we *think* we can't.

"I honestly didn't think I had a choice in my response," Barry mused. "The only mechanism I had for dealing with imperfection was having an outburst. I didn't realize there were options."

Barry's recovery strategy began with his self-talk. I had him write down what he said to himself out on the court. Then I had him pick out a guy on the desk, a junior trader who looked up to him. "Now look at what you've written down," I said to Barry. "Would you talk to him like that?"

For Barry, becoming aware of what he said was the key to freeing himself from the anger reflex that torpedoed his game. We also worked on centering, his pre-event routine, and his focus. Within a month he gained control over himself. And not just on the squash court.

"In retrospect I see how it's made a difference at work too," he says. "Today a floor broker did some trading I didn't agree with, and I lost thirty-two thousand bucks for no reason. It was so stupid! I could feel myself getting tense. Two months ago I would have thrown the phone down—I used to do that *a lot*. But I didn't. I walked away from my desk, went into the conference room, and just sat there, alone, until I calmed myself down.

"Blowing up can feel good for a moment," Barry reflects, "because it's a release. But I paid for it in decreased ability, decreased performance. Now I have a choice. I'm choosing not to lose it. It feels *great*."

Using Anger to Focus Past Distraction

Anger you direct at yourself—whether because you've screwed up or someone else has—is never constructive. Beating yourself up doesn't bring out your best, and it doesn't change what's past.

Yet anger can be enormously constructive—even lifesaving—if directed at an obstacle or circumstance standing between you and your goal.

In 1993 I worked with champion platform diver Russ Bertram—although at that point he'd never even won a national title. Russ was twenty-seven when his coach, Ron O'Brien, introduced us. Unlike everybody else on the team, he'd come to platform diving late, when he was twenty years old. It was his dream, his total passion, to win a national title or international competition before pursuing a "real" career, yet at twenty-seven time was running out. He was putting off his life and career for a vision he could not seem to make happen.

He struggled to make his rent. He needed a win badly—but of course, the more desperately he needed it, the more elusive it became.

All this would have been enough to give Russ the chip on his shoulder his coach described. As it happened, there was something else, something I wouldn't learn about until years later. He'd been sexually molested as a child. But it didn't matter why Russ was angry; he was, and it was getting in the way of what he most wanted, adding to his rage and frustration.

My approach to using anger constructively isn't in the least contingent upon knowing the source or reason for that anger. It doesn't matter *why* you feel the way you do; the point is, you have this emotion roiling your guts and firing your nerve endings, so you may as well use it constructively. Energy like that isn't always available, and it would be a tragic waste to ignore it, squander it, or try to quash it. The trend in modern psychology, I full well realize, is to try to defuse anger by delving into what gave rise to it, in the hope that understanding it puts you in control of it or banishes it altogether. This may be helpful on some level, but in my experience, going into the past to work on what happened there is not any way to fix it. What matters is what you make of the present moment. What matters is how you use what has shaped you in the past to affect the here and now positively—because by acting on the present you get to mold the future.

My job as a performance coach was to get Russ to dive better, not psychoanalyze him. I told him we were going to use his anger to his advantage.

Russ headed into every practice and competition the same way. He began with ten minutes of jump-roping, to get his heart rate up to about 140. Once he had his heart going, he worked on getting himself psyched up. As the diver before him ascended the platform, Russ recalled the source of his anger and let himself pound the wall with his fist. Then he'd breathe and center until he'd lowered his heart rate back to normal, to prove to himself he was in control of his energy and emotions.

At the edge of the platform, Russ would then call up his anger with words. "You can see me mouthing something out there," he says, referring to video footage taken by a camera about ten feet from the platform's edge. "I'm releasing very angry words, because they helped me build what I felt into something razor-sharp, something I could aim like an arrow."

Anger, that is, helped Russ narrow his focus to the dive. "Those intense thoughts and words weren't a distraction, but a shield against distraction," he explains. "They helped me ignore the audience, the TV crew, even the importance of the competition."

Russ won his first national title that year; in 1994 he won his second, and before he retired in 1997, he won several international competitions. But it was by no means easy sailing for Russ. A shoulder injury in 1995 wiped him out for a year, and several times he was hospitalized for an ulcer whose treatment required he go on catabolic steroids (which reduce muscle mass). What propelled him forward, through all the setbacks, was his anger.

"At my age, lesser issues than injury, surgery, and rehab could have brought me into retirement," he reflects. "But eighty, ninety percent of the time, I was able to perform at the top of my game because that channeling process worked so well. It fueled me. I could control my body better. Anger is probably not something you want to tap forever, but it helped me have success when every day I felt like I was teetering on failure."

Like nerves, anger is an energy source. And like nervous energy, it can be harnessed to fuel the concentration, commitment, and physical endurance that performance always requires. Nerves, as I've shown, can power great performances. Anger, I can demonstrate, can be the leverage you use to vault yourself back into action.

When I first came to New York, I worked with an opera singer who simply could not get to first base. He'd lost audition after audition, and with each setback, his anger and frustration mounted, until by the time I met him, he was ready to explode. I didn't question the source of his anger; I put it to use. Instead of telling him to park it, I had him focus on it. I taught him to center; the process cue he chose, which I supported, was "fuck you." He imagined himself saying this to the audition panel as he introduced himself, and again right before he started to sing.

He blew them away with his power. And he got the job.

Since then, I've come to help others utilize their anger and tap its power. The trick is to plant it in your center like a battery—as though you were the Energizer Bunny.

USING ANGER TO POWER A REBOUND

1. **Write down a list of petty annoyances and legitimate angers.** (Steer clear of inventorying out-and-out rage.)

2. **Beginning with the first petty annoyance, imagine it so that you experience it all over again, and then capture this annoyance in your fist.**

3. **Stow it in your center.** Leave it there to fester and ferment.

4. **When you're ready, unleash it.** Use it to its fullest. Bleed the storage tank dry. Leave nothing behind. Expel it totally.

5. If you see positive effects, **work through that list and start in on the legitimate angers.** Each can be a very effective fuel source when you need a big rebound.

This strategy isn't for everyone. If you can't effectively place your anger in your center, or if anger makes you tense key muscle groups, try the approach I used with Jeff Lee. He was a senior at the University of Oklahoma who hadn't won a college golf tournament since he was on the national championship team as a freshman.

Jeff was a kid with a lot of talent. He couldn't put it into play, his coach told me, because he was perpetually one stroke away from exploding. I saw this for myself when I observed him anonymously in tournament play; I also saw why: When Jeff crouched down to line up his putt, there on the other side of the flag, in his line of sight, stood his father, arms folded, eyes locked on his son. When Jeff missed the putt, his father threw a tantrum—and so did Jeff.

I tried to perform a fatherectomy. But since there was no way to do that expeditiously, I coached Jeff on the recovery strategy, with one deviation: Every time he marked his ball on the green and picked it up for the putt, I wanted him to channel some anger into the ball—squeeze it as hard as he could, first with his left hand, then with his right, shaking out each hand as he finished. Then he was to focus the rest of the energy on making the putt. If he was still pissed after walking off the green, he was to try and pulverize the ball all over again. "I'll give you a hundred bucks if you break it," I joked.

Jeff got the idea. He saw the humor in it, which was part of his therapy, but more important, he found his anger working for him instead of against him. Later that year he won his first college tournament by beating future PGA star Phil Mickelson in a play-off.

Developing the Ability to Fight

Anger has gotten a very bad rap in our culture. We no longer differentiate anger from violence, cause from effect. With gun slaying on the rise in our schools, we're on a national campaign to eliminate not just the violence but any outward show of anger. It's quite politically incorrect to suggest that anger be tapped and utilized when government leaders, school administrators, parents, and teachers everywhere are scared to death of it and want it eliminated altogether.

But I maintain that anger is not something you can eliminate. Press it down, deny it exists, insist it exists for the wrong reasons, and it will only bubble up in some unanticipated and perhaps even violent way. We stand a much better chance of controlling violence if we find ways to harness the anger behind it. So much good can come from applying this enormous natural resource if only we acknowledge its value and learn how to channel its power.

My experience in the military made me utterly committed to finding nonviolent solutions to conflict. And yet the military also taught me that anger is often what keeps us from succumbing to adversity. Without it we accept setbacks we should fight to overcome. Without it we are victims. And victims don't shape their future or make their dreams happen.

Upon entering West Point, I was probably the last person you'd describe as a fighter. I received an athletic appointment based on my diving. Yet by the end of my service, I'd learned how to turn on the fighter within me. Even now I can bring forth that fighter in an instant, should circumstances call for it. That doesn't mean I get violent. It simply means I don't accept a situation that denies me the opportunity to give my best. And I don't allow my students or clients to, either. I train them to bring out the fighter within.

Everyone has this fighter. A few individuals seem to require no training to bring it forth. They actually excel under adverse circumstances. The tougher the crowd, or the greater the odds, or the more numerous the difficulties, the more focused they become.

Michelle Mitchell is one of these individuals. I don't believe I ever worked with anyone who fed on adversity the way Michelle did. In 1985, six months after losing the Olympic gold medal to a Chinese diver in Los Angeles, Michelle found herself up against this same woman in the FINA World Cup held in Beijing. Diving was then the fourth most popular sport in China, so the arena in which the competition was held was more like a stadium than aquatic center, and some ten thousand to fifteen thousand Chinese filled the stands. Michelle and her Olympic nemesis were neck and neck; the competition came down to their final dives. The Chinese woman took the platform first and executed a terrific dive, to the wild cheers of her fans.

"I saw her marks, and I knew I had to get solid nines," Michelle recalls.

Michelle was doing her hardest dive—the hardest in the world, in fact: an inward three-and-a-half tuck, which requires you to stand backward on the platform and throw yourself inward toward the tower. As her name and dive were announced, the crowd hushed. But as she assumed her position, Michelle heard stomping feet and then random claps and then a thousand teacups tinkling against stairs and railings and seats.

"At first I thought a fight had broken out in the audience," she says, "but then I realized they were trying to distract me. I thought, *The nerve!* So I said a few expletives, raised my arms, and said to myself, *I'm gonna show them.*"

Michelle nailed the dive—she knew it when she hit the water. The scoreboard would read all nines. But what she didn't expect, when she came out of the water, was total silence. She had hushed the entire audience.

"They had thought I'd crumble," Michelle says. "They didn't know I loved that kind of pressure."

The Chinese officials were highly apologetic. They were embarrassed by the behavior of the audience; their apology to Michelle and their warning to future audiences were carried in all the newspapers, so that 2 billion people knew what Michelle had been up against.

But that only made her victory sweeter.

"It was the neatest thing, to be in Communist China and hear our national anthem played while I stood at the top of the award platform," notes Michelle. "That was the highlight of my career, really—not the Olympics. The satisfaction of standing up against my competitor and that audience—and succeeding—was *huge.*"

Michelle coaches diving now; she's now Michelle Mitchell-Rocha, the head diving coach at the University of Arizona. One of the hardest things, she says, is instilling that hang-tough attitude in her athletes. "It's much easier to teach a skill than an attitude," she observes. Yet she finds that by sharing stories like this one, her athletes begin to incorporate her experience of overcoming adversity as though it were their own. By filling their heads with her real-life Rocky Balboa movies, she is in fact cultivating the fighter in each of them.

Training the Fighter Within

A singer whom we'll call Shelly sought me out to help her win auditions. She was nearing thirty, and she was sick and tired of being eclipsed by younger talent. She was ready to fight for what she felt was her due, but she didn't know how. A divorce had left her feeling victimized. She felt old.

To get Shelly up for the fight, I immersed her in a bath of inspiration. I had her watch *Rocky* movies. Since she lived in Philadelphia at the time, I had her run up and down the steps of the art museum to get herself in a Balboa state of mind. I gave her Jim Loehr's book *The New Toughness Training for Sports*. I told her to get in shape, because I was going to take her to a local gym and go a couple of rounds with her. We didn't actually do that, but the boxing metaphor continued to frame our strategy. She was to envision each audition stage as a boxing ring. Before she went in, she imagined putting on a pair of boxing gloves. Whenever she called me from a foreign city, wracked with prefight doubts and fears, I'd hear her out, and then I'd say, "Are your gloves on? There's the bell!"

Her process cue became "dinggggg!"

When an audition for a major city opera came up, Shelly won the first round despite having to fly from Utah to Los Angeles and sing the same day.

A season later, when she went to Chicago to compete again, Shelly forgot to bring her gloves. She called me and said she didn't feel like fighting anymore. She knew most of the mezzo-sopranos she'd be up against. They were her colleagues. They were really, really good.

"Get your gloves out," I told her. "I know you don't like feeling like you have to tear down your friends to get this job, but this is a competition! You've got to be in fighter mode!"

It wasn't only her colleagues she had to get tough with, either. Fears and doubts, what Shelly called "my ugly stepsisters," were always with her, threatening to tear her down. *You're too old,* they said, shaking their heads. *You're not what they want. Your high notes suck.*

But Shelly imagined putting on her boxing gloves. She also put a rubber band on her wrist—and every time the stepsisters spoke up, she snapped it hard and verbally punched them.

"It was the fight of my life," Shelly told me later, referring to her second and final audition. "I sat in my dressing room and talked to those stepsisters out loud, like a criminal prosecutor. I told myself I'm meant to do this. I'm prepared. I know my music. I'm a singer, and I'm not about to be anything else. Why not me? I deserve this!"

When she got the job, I sent Shelly a pair of real boxing gloves; she sent me back a picture of herself wearing them, in her formal audition gown.

"When the chips are down, I hear you say, 'There's the bell!' and I call up my fighter and put on my gloves," she wrote. "I thought toughness was something you were born with, but it's not: You can develop it. I'm a completely different person. I can be tough. I can compete."

How to Hang Tough

It's one thing to discover you can be a scrapper; it's another to realize you've got to stay in the ring, round after round.

The thing about being in the ring, the fighting never lets up. The punches keep coming. You don't get to put away the gloves. If you're going to last nine rounds or more, you've got to pace yourself. Physically. And mentally.

Over and over, my students who win auditions and get their dream job call me a month or two later, shocked to realize that getting the job is only the beginning: They've got to fight to keep it.

Hope* is an oboist I worked with who recently won a chair with a premier orchestra. Within days of moving to her new city and practicing with her new orchestra, Hope started having problems. She couldn't get her oboe to sound the way she wanted because she couldn't seem to make a reed right anymore. Oboists spend a lot of time making reeds, because factors like humidity and dryness affect the way air passes through them. Hope knew how to carve a reed for the humid Northeast, not the dry Southwest. She couldn't control the weather, so she felt helpless to control her sound. The more she struggled, the more insistently her old fear whispered, *You're going to fail*.

We spoke on the phone. "You've just got to get into that fighter mentality," I told her. "This reed business is like boot camp: You've just got to slog through it. Accept the situation. It's going to be stressful, but you've fought your way through worse. You can do it."

Hope gave herself a goal to work toward: an ideal reed in six weeks. She was on her way to achieving that, focusing on the task in the day-to-day way I'd shown her, when she took another hit. A guest conductor asked her to play a note so that he could tune something for pitch—and nothing came out of her instrument. Hope was mortified. That was in the morning. Later in the day she had to play an exposed part of a violin concerto solo, and her low note cut out. "Second oboe," the conductor said, exasperated, "you're going to have to play it longer."

"Somehow," Hope explained to me later, "I pulled it off. But I came home from that concerto and told myself, *I have to quit. This is too hard. This isn't for me.*"

She didn't call me. But she had the tools, she told me later, and one of them was a list I'd made for her based on things I'd learned at West Point. The list looked like this:

THE PRINCIPLES OF WAR

1. Know your objective.
2. Economize your resources/energy.
3. Always take the offensive or initiative.
4. Stay flexible and responsive to change.

5. Concentrate your fight on one front at a time.

6. Synchronize your forces.

7. Hang in no matter what.

It seemed appropriate to review these principles, said Hope, because she was clearly in the war zone with this concerto. She was going to have to play that exposed part two more times in rehearsal and three more times in actual performance.

"I told myself I was going to get it to work, no matter what I had to do—if I had to use a different reed or stick things in the bell or put on a mute," Hope said. "I wasn't going to let that guest conductor say, 'This is not acceptable,' ever again. I was going to get rested, I was going to play long notes until I got it, I was going to concentrate harder than ever before. *You're going to play this tough part in the first ten minutes of the program,* I told myself, *and no matter what, you're going to nail it.*

"And I did," said Hope.

Mental Toughness

We've talked about a lot of things that get in the way of a great performance. Fear, of course. Self-doubt. An inability to concentrate. Low motivation. Excessive nervous energy. An inability to recover quickly from a mistake.

But what gets in the way of success in the long run?

A desire for perfection.

One great performance is not success; success is a string of great performances. Success is doing your best on command, over and over. Doing your best is tough. Doing it over and over is even tougher.

If you strive to do it perfectly, however, success is downright impossible. No amount of fighter instinct, mental toughness, or anger will change those odds. You will never get what you most want out of life if the standard you apply to the pursuit is perfection.

Legend has it that during the stage run of *Othello* in London, Sir

Laurence Olivier gave a performance one night that was so powerful, so breathtaking, so flawless, that critics rushed to pay phones during intermission to tell every colleague, writer, actor, director, and producer they knew to come over and catch the actor in possibly the performance of a lifetime. When the play was over, and Olivier had retreated from a standing ovation to his dressing room, the press congregated outside his door, hoping to get a quote from the Great One when he emerged. But Olivier didn't come out; it seemed to those who waited that he was having some kind of nervous breakdown. They heard moaning and wailing, shrieking and cursing, the sound of objects being thrown, fists hitting the wall, and, finally, silence.

One of the press knocked timidly on the door. Olivier poked his head out.

"Sir Laurence?" the critic ventured. "What's the matter? Do you know that you delivered probably the best performance in the history of the stage?"

"I know," said Olivier, shaking his head. "It's just that . . . *I have no idea what I did!*"

Perfection is not realistic. Striving for it causes failure. Changing your standard to something slightly less than perfection is not a concession; it's what makes success possible.

Polly Bergen, one of the great stage performers of the fifties and sixties, was forced to learn this the hard way.

Polly could command an audience of two thousand in an instant. It wasn't her voice so much as her charisma. Her interpretation of the lyrics gave her singing its power. For years she enjoyed not only top billing—on Broadway, on television, in Vegas—but a top salary.

In her mid-thirties, however, Polly attended another singer's big opening at Coconut Grove. Polly watched Barbra Streisand, who was all of twenty-one, step out on stage. She listened to her sing. She turned to her husband, who happened to be Streisand's agent, and said, "That kid's automatically doing what it took me until now to learn how to do."

And Polly quit. She got so down on herself she walked away from the stage, her career, and her success. She stopped singing totally. "I didn't sing at parties, I didn't even sing in the shower," she said. "If I couldn't sing the way I wanted—effortlessly, perfectly—then I wasn't going to sing at all."

It wasn't easy.

"I'd hear someone else sing on the stage, and it would absolutely kill me that it wasn't me out there," added Polly. "A couple times I even thought, *I'll go back*. But immediately I'd realize there was no way, because I was an extremely heavy smoker. My voice would be terrible, I thought. So I'd back off."

Nearly thirty-five years passed. Polly got divorced. She moved to Montana. She started a cosmetics business. She lost a fortune. She made one back again. She moved to New York. She quit smoking. And one day, in the mail, as a surprise gift from her goddaughter, she got some tapes of herself performing on television in 1968.

"I watched myself," Polly told me, "and I was cursing myself for stepping down. Because I was *good*. I didn't remember I was that good! And I had walked away!"

Then came the second surprise. She caught herself singing along with the tape. And after eight months off cigarettes, her voice was moderately clear.

Polly got on the phone. She got herself an appointment with one of the best voice teachers in the business, Trish McCaffrey. After forty-five minutes of singing, Polly asked Trish to be brutally honest with her. "Can I get my voice back?" she asked.

Trish looked her in the eye. "I don't see why you won't get it back one hundred percent."

That's when Polly called me for an appointment. As Trish quickly perceived, helping Polly return to the stage wasn't simply a matter of helping her rebuild her voice.

When Polly took the Seven Skills Survey, she scored high in Mental Toughness. She had a strong fighter instinct. She scored low, how-

ever, in Ability to Recover. She foundered on that fifth step of the recovery strategy—the one that says, "Do it good before you try to do
it great." She wanted to make up for the past thirty-five years, not just
go on stage and sing. She wanted to sound like Ella Fitzgerald, not just
return as Polly Bergen. And that was keeping her from coming back
at all.

GETTING PAST PERFECTIONISM

1. **Get your self-talk positive.** We worked on Polly's left-brain
critic, the source of all those absolutist notions like "pass/fail,"
"right/wrong," "perfect/not worth doing." It was particularly fond
of the words "can't" and "never."

2. **Program your mental visuals with highlight films.** I had
Polly reminisce about her great moments on stage—moments that
weren't perfect but stuck out in her mind as high points of her career. I asked her to visualize a night when the song and the energy
just poured out, when the audience was eating out of her hand,
when she felt like a million bucks. Polly had no trouble zeroing in
on just one of these; she came up with tons of them. Time after
time, she discovered, she had controlled an audience with the dy-
namism of her performance, no matter whether her voice had been
"on" or not. She had always known her singing wasn't the thing
that mattered, and looking at these films, she could admit it. She
could see her success had never hinged on perfection. "I really
drew strength from reliving those moments, not only when I was
singing my best but when I wasn't and pulled it off anyway," she
said.

3. **Commit to go for it.** Buoyed by this realization and the
progress she'd made with her voice teacher, Polly accepted a role
in a production of the sixties hit *Company,* a role she felt confident
she could play as an actress. When she got the score, she nearly lost
her nerve. It was an incredibly demanding vocal part. She threw

herself into it, but even when her teacher was satisfied, Polly still wasn't sure. Yet as soon as she walked from the wings into the light, her fears fell away. She proved to herself what she'd always known.

"I can walk out on stage and it doesn't matter if I can sing," she admitted. "I can communicate. I can survive. I always could. No matter what, I'd get through a song, and the audience would love what I was doing. If I could do it once, I realized, I could do it always."

4. Make your imperfections your assets. Not that Polly's given up on trying to sing better. She's still working on her voice. But she has a new attitude toward her imperfections.

"I can't carry a phrase through all the way yet," she explains. "It bugged me at first. I'd run out of air, and there'd be a pause. But I've come to realize that pause brings a whole new interpretation to the song, one that's truer than ever. I used to interpret songs pretty well, but that was all acting. Now it's me. It comes from my life.

"Imperfections are a part of life," she continues. "You take them and use them as part of what you're doing until they're no longer imperfections—they're assets. They make the moment more interesting, funny, dramatic. They're yours. They're something you control, rather than something that controls you."

Unhappiness over not being perfect is still something Polly fights. She was raised to believe that if you couldn't do something perfectly, then you shouldn't do it at all. "I lived that belief for nearly seventy years," she notes. "I'll probably never completely shake it."

But "never" is something Polly is saying less often these days. With every walk she makes from the wings to the light—and she's recently gone in front of audiences from Los Angeles to New York—she gets closer to shedding her fear of being less than perfect.

"This is who I am," says Polly. "The light is where I belong.

The knowledge of that will always carry me through, no matter how fearful I get in the wings."

She reflects a moment—the kind of pause that makes her audience hear the lyrics in a whole new way. "For thirty-five years, I let fear get in the way of me being me. I'm not going to let it rob me of one more day."

SUMMARY

Resilience, the final factor in the success equation, consists of three qualities or skills:

- The ability to recover, quickly, from a mistake, and not bog down in anger
- The ability to fight for what you most want or what you believe in
- Mental toughness, the ability to hang in and persevere no matter what the setback or failure you've suffered

Resilience is a function of resisting the inclination to bog down in anger and remorse. Choosing to move on is easier, however, when we're armed and ready to deal with the inevitable mistakes. Strategies include:

- A basic five-step recovery strategy
- Getting past anger as a distraction
- Using anger to focus
- Harnessing anger to power a rebound
- Finding the fighter within
- Heeding the Principles of War

Because mental toughness is best taught by example, this chapter focuses on individuals who have overcome major setbacks. But they have done so by **getting past perfectionism,** which means:

* Making self-talk positive
* Programming the mind with highlight films
* Making imperfections into assets
* Committing to go for it

You can learn how to incorporate the five-step recovery strategy into your daily life by turning to Appendix G. And now you're ready to put it all together and go for it.

Remember, turn to Appendix G for your own Resilience Plan.

CHAPTER EIGHT

Synthesis: Putting It All Together

Striving for excellence motivates you; striving for perfection is demoralizing.

—DR. HARRIET BRAIKER

If you've been following me from the beginning, you've met quite a few of my clients by now. Each of them has struggled with issues like your own. Each of them has adopted one or more of the strategies explored so far. Each of them has put the program to the test.

Now it's your turn.

I want you to look at your appointment book, Filofax, or Palm Pilot and zero in on some event in the very near future for which you'll need to be in top form. Have you got a deadline threatening? A Little League game to ump? A pitch to make to a new client? A real estate deal you want to close? An investment you've got to decide whether to sell?

Maybe you're interviewing for a job. Maybe you're meeting with a friend in crisis and you really want to say the right thing. Maybe you're presenting your team's findings to the grant review panel. Maybe you just need to confront your baby-sitter about being late again.

There are literally scores of performances throughout the week, throughout each *day,* in which to give your newfound skills a road test. Don't look for an Olympic-sized trial or a national convention to give them a spin. You want to work up to those events. You want to get some practice beforehand, some feedback by which you can refine your skills. You want an opportunity that causes your heart to beat a little faster, not go into seizure.

Once you've got your event picked out—the confrontation or presentation, the decision or negotiation—take a minute to run through the following checklist. It's not a test; it's just a quickie review, a chance to check off all that you need to have dealt with if you're to go out and give your best.

READINESS CHECKLIST

Have you determined your mission?

Are you clear on your goals?

Do you have the energy?

Is it within your control?

Are you confident in your ability and training?

Have you imagined yourself performing well?

Is your self-talk positive?

Are your fears in check?

Do you remember what you wrote in your Courage Journal?

Do you have new entries in your Courage Log?

Are you centered?

Can you focus past distractions?

Have you followed your pre-event routine?

Are you 100 percent committed to giving it your best?

Are you prepared to trust your talent and go for it?

If you feel you're not ready, or that you could be *more* ready, well— join the club. All of us go into performances thinking we could have benefited from one more dry run, one more hour of study, a little more sleep. You have the luxury now of getting more ready: You can go back to the chapters you need to review one more time. You can brush up on the skills you're not so sure you have. But at some point, you need to accept that you're never going to be *perfectly* ready. You've got to stop making excuses. Just commit to doing the best you can.

So go for it. Try to resist evaluating yourself in midperformance. When you're done, when the performance is past, turn the page.

Evaluating Your Performance

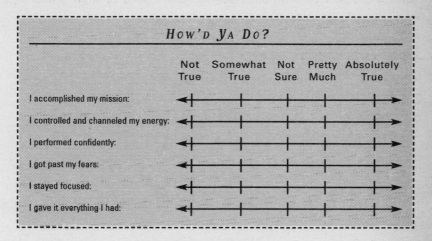

HOW'D YA DO?					
	Not True	Somewhat True	Not Sure	Pretty Much	Absolutely True
I accomplished my mission:					
I controlled and channeled my energy:					
I performed confidently:					
I got past my fears:					
I stayed focused:					
I gave it everything I had:					

Every once in a while you will perform not just well, not just admirably, but at a peak level. You will pull it all together in one magical display. You will tap your full potential. Every bit of your talent will shine. Every bit of your training will show. Every bit of your passion, your commitment, and your dedication will come into play such that you give all that you've got to give, with nothing held back by fear or doubt.

It's a glorious feeling. It makes all the less-than-optimal, all the mediocre, even all failure, seem worth enduring.

But let's understand something about performance: It's not about perfection. It's about playing to your strengths, tapping your talent, and fulfilling your potential. It's not about being flawless—not most of the time, not some of the time, not even occasionally. It may happen that once in your life you pull off a perfect ten. But don't make it your standard. If you strive for perfection instead of excellence, then you are doomed to deny yourself not only great performances but the joy that they can bring.

Ultimately, the brass ring is self-actualization. The goal you should embrace is not necessarily being *the* best, but doing *your* best. If they happen to be one and the same, great. Awesome. Enjoy the privilege; savor the moment, because it's rare and fleeting if it happens at all.

If not—if you can only claim to have done your best—then no matter what the outcome, no matter what your mistakes, you have succeeded. That's the standard I want you to apply to your performances, no matter how small or great, no matter how major or minor the stakes.

Optimal performances, in my book, are those in which you go for it give your all-out best. As long as you do that—as long as you're not beating yourself up in any way for falling short of perfection or short of others' expectations—then I'm satisfied you've learned what I've set out to share with you. I wish you the best.

APPENDIX A

Determination Plan

Week 1

For this week, you'll focus on the four point field order:

Assess the situation ○

Determine your mission ○

Figure out the execution and logistics ○

Prepare for contingencies ○

Time Management

Spend at least a day assessing your situation. At this point, don't spend more than a day on determining your mission, and allow two or three days for the execution and logistics. Finally, give yourself at least a day to consider contingencies. Make sure to set aside the last day for rest, when you do nothing but reward yourself for having accomplished these activities.

Week 2

For this week, you'll concentrate on the bubble and funeral exercises, which comprise seven activities:

Brainstorming ideas   ◯
Editing them down   ◯
Living with your bubble for a day   ◯
Revising your bubble as necessary   ◯
Choosing the location of your funeral   ◯
Imagining the service   ◯
Processing your insights   ◯

Time Management

Allow a day or more to brainstorm your ideas for the bubble. Give yourself an entirely new day to edit down your list. Budget a day or two for revision—you may not get it right the first time. It's only going to take a day to give yourself the time to imagine your funeral. But expect that it will take several days to reflect and process on what the exercise has shown you. Remember to save one day at the end of the week for rest and reward.

Week 3

This week, you'll complete your goal map. This consists of four activities:

Setting up your time frame   ◯
Writing in your mission   ◯
Figuring out your execution   ◯
Working out the logistics   ◯

Time Management

Filling in the time frame and mission should require less than a day. You'll spend the bulk of your week mapping out a week-to-week or month-to-month strategy. Remember to set aside at least a day for rest and rewards.

APPENDIX B

Energy Plan

Week 1

For this week, you'll focus on proper abdominal breathing, the pre-requisite to Centering Down:

Lying Down   O
Sitting   O
Standing   O

Time Management

Spend the first few days practicing breathing when lying down, for one or two minutes at a time. Repeat this, and the rest of the Centering exercises, three to seven times a day. Allow another day or two to make sure that you're able to breathe properly in a sitting position. Spend the remainder of the week practicing while standing. Make sure to set aside the last day for rest, when you do nothing but reward yourself for having accomplished these activities.

Week 2

For this week, we'll concentrate on learning to Center Down, involving seven activities:

Forming your clear intention   O
Picking a focal point   O
Breathing mindfully   O
Releasing tension   O
Finding your center   O
Repeating your process cue   O
Directing your energy   O

Time Management

Your intention will be to learn to Center. After you pick your point, begin proper breathing. Check for tension in your key muscles. Do this for a day or two, until you can get your key muscles relatively relaxed in less than seven breaths. Give yourself at least two days to find your center in seven breaths or less. Spend a day or two trying out different process cues and directing your energy. Remember to save the last day for rest and reward.

Week 3

This week, you'll work on honing your ability to Center Down in less time:

Centering in one minute or more   O
Centering in 20–45 seconds   O
Centering in 10 seconds or less   O

Time Management

Spend the first day or two Centering with as many as 3–5 breaths for any of the steps. Then start practicing with less breaths, especially for mindful breathing, releasing tension and finding your center. Finally, try Centering in four breaths: the first is for your clear intention and focal point; the second for mindful breathing and releasing tension; the third to be at your center; then say your process cue and direct your energy to your point. Remember to save at least one day for rest and rewards.

APPENDIX C

Perspective Plan

Week 1

For this week, you'll focus on becoming aware of your Self-Talk and boosting your Self-Confidence by:

Monitoring your self-talk   ◯
Writing down the negative   ◯
Taking right actions   ◯
Stockpiling small successes   ◯

Time Management

Spend the first few days monitoring your inner dialogue and capturing all the negative language on paper. Then start doing the right thing and achieving small successes. Make sure to set aside the last day for rest, when you do nothing but reward yourself for having accomplished these activities.

Week 2

For this week, we'll concentrate on changing your Self-Talk, which involves four activities:

Personifying the voices   O
Talking back to the critics   O
Writing out affirmations   O
Reprogramming your self-talk   O

Time Management

Start with last week's notes from your inner critics. One by one, personify each of negative voices and challenge their accusations or criticisms. Do this for a few days, until you have an answer for each of them. Take a day or two to write out your affirmations, then spend the next few days changing the language of your inner dialogue. Remember to set aside a day for rest and reward.

Week 3

This week, you'll work on your Expectancy, which involves three activities:

Examining doomsday videos   O
Reprogramming with highlight films   O
Mentally rehearsing   O

Time Management

Use the first day to examine the tragic movies before replacing them. Then allow at least two days to reprogram them with better images. Spend several days practicing mental rehearsal, once or twice a day. Remember to save at least a day for rest and rewards.

APPENDIX D

Courage Plan

Week 1

This week, you'll focus on courageous actions. This includes three activities:

Completing your Courage Journal   O
Noting courageous actions   O
Dealing with your zingers   O

Time Management

Spend a day or two reflecting on past acts of courage. Then begin looking for opportunities to act courageously. Keep track of your actions and how you deal with the zingers. Make sure to set aside the last day for rest, when you do nothing but reward yourself for having accomplished these activities.

Week 2

For this week, you'll concentrate on three courage-building activities:

Practicing assertiveness   O
Acting as if   O
Using your humor   O

Time Management

Spend a day or two rehearsing your assertiveness scripts. Use the remainder of the week to try them out, as well as acting "as if." Keep noting all your courageous actions. Try flexing your sense of humor every day. Remember to save a day for rest and reward.

Week 3

This week, you'll work on further strengthening your courage, which involves seven activities:

Writing out fears of success   O
Completing your Courage Log   O
Surrounding yourself with symbols   O

Time Management

Use the first day or two examining your fears of success and how you'll handle them. Spend the next several days completing the courage entries and acquiring symbols of your courageous acts. Remember to save at least a day for rest and rewards.

APPENDIX E

Focus Plan

Week 1

This week, you'll begin working on your focus, which consists of four activities:

Eliminating external distractions ○
Creating an attentional boundary ○
Allocating your energy ○
Centering for presence ○

Time Management

Spend a few days writing out all the distractions and constructing your attentional boundary. Use one day to figure out how to allocate your energy wisely, then begin centering for presence, 3–7 times a day. Make sure to set aside the last day for rest, when you do nothing but reward yourself for having accomplished these activities.

Week 2

This week, you'll be intensifying your focus, which involves five activities:

Centering Up   O
Visualizing   O
Sustaining visual focus   O
Sustaining auditory focus   O
Sustaining kinesthetic focus   O

Time Management

Starting the first two or three days, practice Centering Up and visualization several times a day. Then spend at least one day on each of the duration exercises. Remember to save the last day for rest and reward.

Week 3

This week, you'll work towards ultimate focus, which involves three activities:

Sustaining focus under adverse conditions   O
Using your pre-event routine   O
Achieving mental quiet   O

Time Management

Use the first two days to complete the adversity training. Spend at least three days finalizing your pre-event routine and working on mental quiet. Remember to save at least one day at the end for rest and rewards.

APPENDIX F

Poise Plan

Week 1

This week, you'll work on decision making and negotiations, which consist of four activities:

Developing a pre-decision routine   O
Getting creative   O
Applying mind mapping   O
Practicing negotiations   O

Time Management

Spend the first day or two working on your pre-decision routine, then use it throughout the week. Take two days to get creative and apply mind mapping to your negotiations. Then practice negotiating deals for the remainder of the week. Make sure to set aside the last day for rest, when you do nothing but reward yourself for having accomplished these activities.

Week 2

For this week, you'll concentrate on making presentations, which involves four activities:

Mind mapping your speeches   O
Directing your focus   O
Acting out your stories   O
Staying in the here and now   O

Time Management

Use a day or two to mind map several speeches. Then spend the remainder of the week delivering them, working on directing your focus, acting out your stories, and staying in the here and now. Remember to save the last day for rest and reward.

Week 3

This week, you'll focus on multitasking, which involves three activities:

Assessing your concentration   O
Getting the monkey off your back   O
Using process cues to speed shifts   O

Time Management

Assess your concentration first and then spend a few days getting the monkey off your back. Take another two or three days to find process cues that speed your shifts. Remember to save at least one day at the end for rest and rewards.

APPENDIX G

Resilience Plan

Week 1

This week, you'll focus on your ability to recover, which consists of four activities:

Five-step recovery strategy   ○
Using anger to focus past distractions   ○
Using anger to power a rebound   ○
Getting past anger   ○

Time Management

Spend the first two days learning the recovery strategy, and then practice it often. Take two or three days to experiment with using anger constructively, and at least one day to write out and change the language of your self-talk. Make sure to set aside the last day for rest, when you do nothing but reward yourself for having accomplished these activities.

Week 2

For this week, you'll work on your ability to fight and mental toughness, which involves three activities:

Finding the fighter within   O
Training the fighter   O
Heeding the principles of war   O

Time Management

Spend a few days reflecting on tough situations and how you fought your way out of them. Consider practicing a martial art or at least watching a *Rocky* or Bruce Lee video. Take two or three days to apply the principles of war to your toughest battles. Remember to save the last day for rest and reward.

Week 3

This final week, you'll concentrate on getting past perfectionism, which involves four activities:

Getting your self-talk positive   O
Programming highlight films   O
Making your imperfections your assets   O
Committing to go for it   O

Time Management

Spend the first two or three days to make sure that your self-talk is positive and that you're viewing only highlight films. Use a day or two considering your imperfections and how to make them work for you. Reserve the next to last day to form your commitment. Remember to save at least one day at the end for rest and rewards.

APPENDIX H

Seven Skills Scoring Instructions

1. Go back to the Seven Skills Survey and change your responses for questions 31 to 77 as follows:

$$1 \to 5 \qquad 2 \to 4 \qquad 4 \to 2 \qquad 5 \to 1$$

Examples:

2. To determine the category score, add your corrected responses

31. $\underline{1} \to 5$
32. $\underline{2} \to 4$
33. $\underline{3} \to 3$

75. $\underline{5} \to 1$
76. $\underline{4} \to 2$
77. $\underline{3} \to 3$

(from 31–77) to your unchanged responses (from 1–30 and 78–96). For example:

INTRINSIC MOTIVATION
1. __4__ 13. __2__ 76. __4 → 2__ 77. __3 → 3__   Total: __11__

COMMITMENT
2. __3__ 3. __2__ 74. __2 → 4__ 75. __5 → 1__   Total: __10__

WILL TO SUCCEED
17. __2__ 72. __1 → 5__ 89. __3__ 91. __2__   Total: __12__

3. The skill score is the sum of its category scores, except for Energy. In this example the skill score for Determination would be 33 (11 + 10 + 12 = 33). Please see below to calculate your Energy score.

4. Go ahead to the Seven Skills Profile on page 225 and circle your skill and category scores on your Profile.

DETERMINATION	12 15 18 21 24 27 30 ㉝ 36 39 42 45 48 51 54 57 60
INTRINSIC	
MOTIVATION	4 5 6 7 8 9 10 ⑪ 12 13 14 15 16 17 18 19 20
COMMITMENT	4 5 6 7 8 9 ⑩ 11 12 13 14 15 16 17 18 19 20
WILL TO SUCCEED	4 5 6 7 8 9 10 11 ⑫ 13 14 15 16 17 18 19 20

DETERMINATION

INTRINSIC MOTIVATION
1. ____   13. ____   76. ____ ____   77. ____ ____   Total: _____

COMMITMENT
2. ____   3. ____   74. ____ ____   75. ____ ____   Total: _____

WILL TO SUCCEED
17. ____   72. ____ ____   89. ____   91. ____   Total: _____

                            Determination Total: _____

ENERGY

OPTIMAL ENERGY
20. ___   21. ___   37. ___ ___   48. ___ ___   Total: _____

PERFORMANCE ENERGY
5. ___   29. ___   30. ___   64. ___ ___   Total: _____

ABILITY TO ENERGIZE
6. ___   19. ___   71. ___ ___   80. ___ ___   Total: _____

ABILITY TO RELAX
36. ___ ___   39. ___ ___   42. ___ ___   51. ___ ___   Total: _____

If Optimal Energy total is greater than Performance Energy total: subtract Performance Energy from Optimal Energy.

Optimal Energy   _____
- Performance Energy   _____
Energy Difference   _____

Subtract the Energy Difference from 20:

                     20
- Energy Difference   _____
Gap Score   _____

Add the Gap Score to your Ability to Energize total. This is your Energy Score.

Gap Score   _____
+ Ability to Energize   _____
Total   _____

                     Energy = _____

Circle this number on your Profile.

If Performance Energy total is greater than or equal to Optimal Energy total: subtract Optimal Energy from Performance Energy.

Performance Energy _____

\- Optimal Energy _____

Energy Difference _____

Subtract the Energy Difference from 20:

20

\- Energy Difference _____

Gap Score _____

Add the Gap Score to your Ability to Relax total. This is your Energy Score.

Gap Score _____

\+ Ability to Relax _____

Total _____

Energy = _____

Circle this number on your Profile.

PERSPECTIVE

SELF-CONFIDENCE

4. ___ 8. ___ 45. ___ ___ 50. ___ ___ Total: _____

SELF-TALK

23. ___ 58. ___ ___ 68. ___ ___ 69. ___ ___ Total: _____

EXPECTANCY

7. ___ 34. ___ ___ 40. ___ ___ 83. ___ Total: _____

Perspective Total: _____

COURAGE

ABILITY TO RISK
15. ___   35. ___ ___   52. ___ ___   95. ___   Total: _____

ABILITY TO RISK DEFEAT
33. ___ ___   46. ___ ___   82. ___   87. ___   Total: _____

ABILITY TO RISK SUCCESS
16. ___   38. ___ ___   73. ___ ___   90. ___   Total: _____

Courage Total: _____

FOCUS

PRESENCE
27. ___   60. ___ ___   62. ___ ___   93. ___   Total: _____

INTENSITY
25. ___ ___   55. ___ ___   63. ___ ___   92. ___   Total: _____

DURATION
61. ___ ___   65. ___ ___   66. ___ ___   96. ___   Total: _____

MENTAL QUIET
26. ___   57. ___ ___   59. ___ ___   94. ___   Total: _____

Focus Total: _____

POISE

DECISION MAKING
22. ___   47. ___ ___   49. ___ ___   85. ___   .   Total: _____

NEGOTIATING
9. ___   10. ___   41. ___ ___   86. ___ ___   Total: _____

PRESENTING
11. ___   12. ___   31. ___ ___   32. ___ ___   Total: _____

MULTITASKING
14. ___   54. ___ ___   56. ___ ___   88. ___   Total: _____

Poise Total: _____

RESILIENCE

ABILITY TO RECOVER
67. ___ ___   70. ___ ___   78. ___   84. ___   Total: _____

ABILITY TO FIGHT
28. ___   43. ___ ___   44. ___ ___   79. ___   Total: _____

MENTAL TOUGHNESS
18. ___   24. ___   53. ___ ___   81. ___   Total: _____

Resilience Total: _____

Seven Skills Profile

	Low	Midrange	High
DETERMINATION	12 15 18 21 24 27	30 33 36 39 42	45 48 51 54 57 60
INTRINSIC			
MOTIVATION	4 5 6 7 8 9	10 11 12 13 14	15 16 17 18 19 20
	Unclear Goals		Driven
COMMITMENT	4 5 6 7 8 9	10 11 12 13 14	15 16 17 18 19 20
	Other Interests		Committed
WILL TO SUCCEED	4 5 6 7 8 9	10 11 12 13 14	15 16 17 18 19 20
	Unimportant		Strong
ENERGY	8 10 12 14 16 18	20 22 24 26 28	30 32 34 36 38 40
OPTIMAL ENERGY	4 5 6 7 8 9	10 11 12 13 14	15 16 17 18 19 20
	Best Calm		Best Up
PERFORMANCE			
ENERGY	4 5 6 7 8 9	10 11 12 13 14	15 16 17 18 19 20
	Relaxed		Up/Anxious
ABILITY TO			
ENERGIZE	4 5 6 7 8 9	10 11 12 13 14	15 16 17 18 19 20
	Difficulty Getting Up		Able to Raise Energy
ABILITY TO RELAX	4 5 6 7 8 9	10 11 12 13 14	15 16 17 18 19 20
	Difficulty Relaxing		Able to Lower Energy
PERSPECTIVE	12 15 18 21 24 27	30 33 36 39 42	45 48 51 54 57 60
SELF-CONFIDENCE	4 5 6 7 8 9	10 11 12 13 14	15 16 17 18 19 20
	Doubting		Confident
SELF-TALK	4 5 6 7 8 9	10 11 12 13 14	15 16 17 18 19 20
	Critical		Supportive
EXPECTANCY	4 5 6 7 8 9	10 11 12 13 14	15 16 17 18 19 20
	Negative		Positive

Seven Skills Profile (cont.)

	Low	Midrange	High
	←		→
COURAGE	12 15 18 21 24 27	30 33 36 39 42	45 48 51 54 57 60
ABILITY TO RISK	4 5 6 7 8 9	10 11 12 13 14	15 16 17 18 19 20
	Cautious		Go for It
ABILITY TO RISK			
DEFEAT	4 5 6 7 8 9	10 11 12 13 14	15 16 17 18 19 20
	Tenative		Courageous
ABILITY TO RISK			
SUCCESS	4 5 6 7 8 9	10 11 12 13 14	15 16 17 18 19 20
	Fear Success		Embrace It
FOCUS	16 20 24 28 32 36	40 44 48 52 56	60 64 68 72 76 80
PRESENCE	4 5 6 7 8 9	10 11 12 13 14	15 16 17 18 19 20
	Elsewhere		Here and Now
INTENSITY	4 5 6 7 8 9	10 11 12 13 14	15 16 17 18 19 20
	Weak		Powerful
DURATION	4 5 6 7 8 9	10 11 12 13 14	15 16 17 18 19 20
	Short		Until Done
MENTAL QUIET	4 5 6 7 8 9	10 11 12 13 14	15 16 17 18 19 20
	Noisy		Quiet
POISE	16 20 24 28 32 36	40 44 48 52 56	60 64 68 72 76 80
DECISION MAKING	4 5 6 7 8 9	10 11 12 13 14	15 16 17 18 19 20
	Confused		Think Clearly
NEGOTIATING	4 5 6 7 8 9	10 11 12 13 14	15 16 17 18 19 20
	Limited		Skilled
PRESENTING	4 5 6 7 8 9	10 11 12 13 14	15 16 17 18 19 20
	Ineffective		Speak Well
MULTITASKING	4 5 6 7 8 9	10 11 12 13 14	15 16 17 18 19 20
	Overwhelmed		Juggle Well

Seven Skills Profile (cont.)

	Low	Midrange	High

RESILIENCE 12 15 18 21 24 27   30 33 36 39 42   45 48 51 54 57 60

ABILITY TO
RECOVER   4 5 6 7 8 9   10 11 12 13 14   15 16 17 18 19 20
   Delayed   Immediate

ABILITY TO FIGHT 4 5 6 7 8 9   10 11 12 13 14   15 16 17 18 19 20
   Victim   Fighter

MENTAL
TOUGHNESS   4 5 6 7 8 9   10 11 12 13 14   15 16 17 18 19 20
   Sensitive   Tough